Slow Cooker Recipes: 200 Healthy Vegetarian Slow Cooker Recipes

Gina 'The Veggie Goddess' Matthews

Copyright

Copyright © 2014 by Gina 'The Veggie Goddess' Matthews

Cover and internal design © by Gina 'The Veggie Goddess' Matthews

All rights reserved. No part of this book may be reproduced in any form, or by any electronic or mechanical means, including information storage and retrieval systems, except in the case of brief quotations in articles or reviews, without permission in writing from the author, Gina 'The Veggie Goddess' Matthews.

Any brand names and product names mentioned within this book are trademarks, registered trademarks, or trade names of their respective holders. The author is not associated with any product or vendor mentioned within this book.

ISBN-10: 1495360385
ISBN-13: 978-1495360381

TABLE OF CONTENTS

INTRODUCTION 1

CHAPTER 1 – SLOW COOKER RECIPES: BREAKFASTS 3

    Breakfast Pudding with Streusel Style Topping..5

    Pecan Crusted French Toast Bake 6

    Breakfast Dumplin's and Mock Sausage Gravy 7

    Mock Ham, Gouda and Potato Bake 9

    Lemon Scone Breakfast Bread 10

    Spinach and Mozzarella Breakfast Frittata...12

    Overnight Apricots and Cream Oatmeal 13

    Stacked Mexican Tortilla Breakfast Casserole...14

    Pumpkin and Berry Breakfast Bread 15

    Southwestern Veggie Omelet and Potato Bake..17

    Design Your Own Mock Sausage Quiche 18

    Overnight Pear and Nut Oatmeal..19

    Vegetarian Ham, Brie and Focaccia Brunch Bake 20

    Southern Green Chile and Jalapeno Grits...21

    French Toast Souffle 22

    Overnight Cocoa and Coconut Oatmeal 23

    Mock Ham and Veggie Quiche 23

    Caramel Pecan Hawaiian Sweet Bread Breakfast Bake 25

    Layered Breakfast Brunch Bake 26

    Banana Nut Bread Oatmeal 27

    Apple Pie Sticky Breakfast Bread 28

    Overnight Breakfast Casserole 29

    Sweet Chai Tea Breakfast Cake 30

    Stacked Challah Bread Vanilla and Almond French Toast 32

    Overnight Trail Mix Oatmeal 33

CHAPTER 2 – SLOW COOKER RECIPES: APPETIZERS 35

    Super Easy Spinach and Artichoke Dip 37

Cheesy Beer Fondue 38
Bean and Cheese Dip 39
Sweet and Spicy Meatballs 40
Spicy Chile Cheese Dip 40
Mock Pigs in a Bac'n Blanket Bites 41
Veggie Pizza Dip 42
Marinated Mushrooms 42
Thick and Spicy Mock Beef and Cheese Dip 43
Caramel Rum Dip 44
Mock Barbecue Kielbasa Bites 45
Spiked Caramel Fondue 45
Chick'n Nachos 46
Mediterranean Bean Dip 47
Sweet and Spicy Mock Kielbasa Bites 48
Spicy Artichoke Zucchini Spread 48
Pizza Fondue 49
Southwestern Style Spinach Dip 50
German Style Kielbasa Bites 51
Party Favorite Vegetarian Cocktail Meatballs 52
Tex Mex Corn Dip 53

CHAPTER 3 – SLOW COOKER RECIPES: SOUPS 55

Minestrone Soup 57
Veggie and Green Lentil Soup 58
Creamy Mushroom Soup 59
Velvety Spiced Pumpkin Soup 60
Layered Split Pea Soup 61
Hot and Sour Soup with Mushrooms 61
Easy Potato Leek Soup 63
Barley and Veggie Soup 64
Mexican-Style Minestrone 65
Zesty Quinoa, Potato and Corn Chowder 66
Jamaican Soup 67
Zesty Black Bean Soup 68
Mexican Style Gumbo 70

Lentil and Rice Soup 71
Easy Garden Soup 72
Black Beans and Rice Soup 73
Easy Navy Bean Soup 75
Taco Soup 76
Mock Ham and Split Pea Soup 77
Creamy Country Succotash Chowder 78
Chipotle and Citrus Black Bean Soup 79
Creamy Italian Tomato Basil Soup 80
Hearty Mock Beef and Broccoli Soup 81
Creole Mock Kielbasa, Greens and Veggie Soup 82
Cheesy Cauliflower Soup 84
Easy Creamy Mushroom Soup 85

CHAPTER 4 – SLOW COOKER RECIPES: STEWS 87

Eggplant, Tomato and Bean Stew 89
Easy Veggie Stew 90
Basic Greek Stew 91
African Yam and Bean Stew 92
Barley Stew 93
Millet and Veggie Stew 94
Moroccan Squash Stew 95
Potato and Black Eyed Pea Stew 96
Nothing but Veggies Stew 97
Hearty Lentil and Veggie Stew 98
Curried Coconut Squash and Chickpea Stew 100
Zesty Southwest Style Bean and Quinoa Stew 101
Asian-Inspired Stew 102
Classic Veggie Stew 103
Beans, Greens and Potato Stew 105
Italian Eggplant and Tomato Stew 106
Layered Potato and Veggie Stew 107
Veggie and Chickpea Stew 109
Italian Eggplant and Zucchini Stew 110
Hearty Winter Stew 111

Gypsy Stew 112

Layered Mushroom and Potato Stew 114

Tex-Mex Tempeh and Black Bean Stew 115

Polynesian Stew 116

Curried Chickpea, Potato and Veggie Stew 117

CHAPTER 5 – SLOW COOKER RECIPES: CHILIS 121

Spicy Chipotle Chocolate Chili 123

Cowboy Chipotle Chili 125

Sweet and Nutty Veggie and Bean Chili 126

Thick and Chunky Zesty Chili 127

Taco Style Chili 128

Three Bean Spicy Cajun Chili 130

Sweet and Spicy Pumpkin Chili 131

Southern Style Chili 132

Tex-Mex Mock Beef Chili 133

Jamaican Black-Eyed Pea Chili 134

Zesty Pumpkin, Pinto and Veggie Chili 135

Spicy Red Bean and Veggie Chili 136

Sweet and Chunky Hominy, Bean and Mock Beef Chili 138

Smoked Bac'Un and Bean Chili 139

Easy Go-To Mock Meat Chili 140

Chunky Chick'n and Green Chile Chili 142

Mock Beef and Chorizo Chili 143

Lentil and Red Bean Chili 144

Mock Turkey and Bean Chili 146

Mock Picante Beef and Bean Chili 147

Chick'n Enchilada Chili 149

White Bean and Veggie Chili 150

Chick'n - Jalapeno Popper Chili 151

Fireside Chili 153

Hot and Hearty Mock Meat Lovers Chili 154

CHAPTER 6 – SLOW COOKER RECIPES: SIDES 157

Caribbean Style Black Beans 159

Indian Lentils and Rice 160

Cracked Wheat Pilaf 161
Moroccan Cauliflower and Potatoes 161
Honey Ginger Lentils 162
Easy Creamed Corn 163
Spicy Coconut Baked Beans 164
Stuffed Roasted Squash 165
Sweet and Spicy Vegetables 166
Wild Rice and Veggie Medley 167
Rich and Velvety Mac and Cheese 168
Zesty Refried Beans 169
Sweet Roasted Autumn Harvest Medley 170
Baked Potatoes 171
Vegan Stuffing 171
Seasoned Zucchini 173
Layered Beans and Barley 174
Southwest Style Pinto Beans 175
Easy Roasted Vegetables 175
Spanish Brown Rice 177
Curried Chickpeas with Vegetables 178
Barley Medley 179
Zesty Southwest Red Beans 180
Spiced Sweet Potatoes and Apples 181
Cheesy Potatoes with Veggies 182
Pineapple Barbeque Baked Beans 183
Spicy Picante Style Lentil and Tomatoes 184
Sweet and Savory Cabbage 185

CHAPTER 7 – SLOW COOKER RECIPES: DESSERTS 187
Red and Blue Berry Cobbler 189
Spruced Up Coconut Rice Pudding 190
Caramel Glazed Pears 191
Nutty Chocolate on Chocolate Brownies 192
Apple Pie Crisp 193
Chocolate Lava Cake 194
Easy Rum Bread Pudding 196

Spiced Applesauce 197

Coconut, Apricot and Pecan Rice Pudding 198

Chocolate Cake 199

Chocolate Cherry Bread Pudding 200

Amaretto Spiked Fruit Compote 201

Nut and Raisin Stuffed Apples 202

Pumpkin, Raisin and Walnut Bread Pudding 203

Candied Pecans 204

Spiced Scone Pudding 205

Tropical Banana Rum Medley 206

Dressed Up Caramel Baked Pears 207

Cinnamon-Raisin Bread and Chocolate Chip Pudding 208

Spiced Apple Cake 209

Decadent Tiramisu Bread Pudding 210

Coconut Apple Crumble 211

Anytime of the Year Pumpkin Pie Pudding 212

Spiced Stewed Apples 213

Amaretto Cherry Cobbler 214

CHAPTER 8 – SLOW COOKER RECIPES: MISCELLANEOUS MAINS ... 217

Lasagna with Vegetarian Meat Substitute 219

Southwest Style Stuffed Peppers 220

Mock Kielbasa, Pineapple and Bean Medley 221

Rice and Veggie Medley 222

Marinara and Pesto Spinach Lasagna 223

Tofu in Sweet and Spicy Peanut Sauce 224

Fajitas Filling Mixture 225

Burrito Filling Mixture 226

Taco Filling Mixture 228

Southwest Enchiladas 229

Layered Italian Polenta and Bean Bake 230

Asian Infused Tofu and Vegetables 231

Creole Jambalaya 233

German Style Mock Sausage, Sauerkraut and Potatoes 234

Lentil Barbeque 235

Lentil and Vegetable Stroganoff 236
Zesty Barbeque Tofu 237
Creamy Artichoke Linguine 238
Sweet and Tangy Mock Barbecue Beef 239
Veggie Spaghetti Sauce 240
German Style Sausage and Sauerkraut 241
Mock Chickn' and Dumplings 242
Seitan Italian "Beef" Sandwiches 243
Mock Italian Sausage and Feta Cheese Stuffed Peppers 244
Sweet and Sour Chick'n 245

SLOW COOKER COOKING TIPS 247

AVAILABLE BOOKS BY AUTHOR: 251

ABOUT THE AUTHOR 253

Introduction

Whether you're cooking for yourself, your family or for a party or large gathering, slow cooker meal preparation is a great way to serve up healthy, delicious and easy to prepare dishes and meals. With nothing more than a little bit of food prep, such as chopping of ingredients or a quick sauté of onions, the remainder of your dish or meal's cooking time is all done by your kitchen appliance, the beloved and trustworthy slow cooker. And, with modern day life being as hectic as it is, juggling family, school, work and other activities, slow cooker meal preparation allows you to prepare healthy meals for you and your family even when time is limited.

Whether you are new to slow cooker meal preparation or a real slow cooker pro, I invite you to browse through the closing chapter that outlines some slow cooker cooking tips helping to make all of your slow cooker dishes a super success.

Bon Veggie Appetit!

Gina "The Veggie Goddess" Matthews

GINA 'THE VEGGIE GODDESS' MATTHEWS

Chapter 1 –
Slow Cooker Recipes: Breakfasts

Gina 'The Veggie Goddess' Matthews

Breakfast Pudding with Streusel Style Topping

Ingredients:

1 cup milk (regular or non-dairy - I use coconut or almond milk for this recipe)

2 cups water

2-1/2 tablespoons pure maple syrup (any grade)

1/2 cup chia seeds (adds superior nutrition and thickens the pudding)

2 tablespoons arrowroot powder (may also use tapioca starch or cornstarch)

1 teaspoon ground cinnamon

pinch of sea salt

5 large apples, any variety (cut into thin slices)

Streusel Style Topping

1/2 cup almond flour (may also use all-purpose flour)

1/4 cup coconut sugar (may substitute with raw sugar)

1/4 cup finely shredded coconut (unsweetened)

1 teaspoon ground cinnamon

1/4 cup natural applesauce (unsweetened)

1 teaspoon pure vanilla extract

In a mixing bowl, stir together the milk, water, maple syrup, chia seeds, arrowroot powder, cinnamon and sea salt until well combined. Spread the mixture into the bottom of your slow cooker and evenly top with the sliced apples, but do not stir or mix them into the underneath layer.

In a separate mixing bowl, stir together all of the topping ingredients until well combined. Evenly crumble and spread the topping mixture on top of the apple layer. Cook on "low" for 4 hours, or if you're in a hurry, cook on "high" for 2 hours. After suggested cooking time, unplug your slow cooker and <u>let the pudding sit, covered, for 1 hour before serving</u>. This is obviously not a breakfast you can make on busy school and work day mornings, but it is easy and great for weekend breakfasts and anytime brunches. Makes 6-8 servings.

Pecan Crusted French Toast Bake

Ingredients:

1 loaf of cinnamon bread (cubed)

3-1/2 cups milk (regular or non-dairy)

1/2 cup raw sugar

3 large eggs (well beaten)

1 tablespoon pure vanilla extract

1 teaspoon ground cinnamon

1/2 teaspoon ground nutmeg

1/4 teaspoon sea salt

Pecan Crust Topping

1/2 cup finely chopped pecans (I run mine through my bullet

blender for a couple of seconds)

2 tablespoons all-purpose flour

2 tablespoons brown sugar

2 tablespoons stick butter (regular or vegan)

In a mixing bowl, whisk together the milk, raw sugar, eggs, vanilla extract, cinnamon, nutmeg and sea salt until well blended. Add in the cubed cinnamon bread and toss until very evenly coated. Cover and let sit in the fridge for 1-4 hours.

Lightly oil the bottom and sides of your slow cooker, spoon in the marinated bread mixture and cook on "low" for 6-8 hours.

To make the pecan crust topping, stir together all of the topping ingredients in a small mixing bowl, using a fork to "cut" in the butter until it resembles wet sand. Uncover your slow cooker during the last 30 minutes of cooking time, crumble in the topping mixture and continue cooking uncovered until all of the excess milk is absorbed. Makes 4-6 servings.

Breakfast Dumplin's and Mock Sausage Gravy

Ingredients:

3 tablespoons olive oil

2 yellow onions (diced)

2 pounds of veggie crumbles

1/4 cup all-purpose flour

2 fresh garlic cloves (minced)

3 cups plain milk (regular or non-dairy)

1-1/2 teaspoons crushed fennel seeds

1-1/2 teaspoons dried sage

1/2 teaspoon ground black pepper

(dumplin's)

3/4 cup all-purpose flour

1/2 cup cornmeal

1 teaspoon aluminum-free baking powder

1/4 teaspoon sea salt

1 large egg

1/3 cup plain milk (regular or non-dairy)

3 tablespoons melted butter

* fresh chopped parsley for garnish

Grease the bottom and sides of your slow cooker with olive oil.

Heat the olive oil in a large saucepan or deep skillet over medium heat. Add in the diced onions and veggie crumbles and cook while stirring frequently until onions become translucent, about 5-6 minutes. Stir in the minced garlic and stir continuously until fragrant, about 30-60 seconds. Stir in the 1/4 cup flour, 3 cups of milk and spices and cook until mixture thickens. Be sure to keep heat at medium or medium-low during cooking time to properly thicken the mock sausage gravy. Transfer mixture into your prepared slow cooker and cook on "low" for 3 hours.

To prepare the dumplin' mixture, whisk together the 3/4 cup flour, cornmeal, baking powder and sea salt. In a separate small mixing bowl whisk together the egg, milk and melted butter and once blended pour into bowl with flour-cornmeal mixture and stir to even blend batter. Lightly oil hands and form 8 dumplin's. After 3 hours of cooking time, drop the dumplin's on top of the mock sausage gravy and cook for an additional 30 minutes, or until toothpick comes out clean from center of dumplin's. Serve with a sprinkle of fresh chopped parsley. Makes 8 servings.

Mock Ham, Gouda and Potato Bake

Ingredients:

6 large eggs

1/2 cup plain milk (regular or non-dairy)

1/4 teaspoon ground black pepper

2 tablespoons butter

3 tablespoons all-purpose flour

1/2 cup vegetable broth

1/2 cup plain milk (regular or non-dairy)

pinch of sea salt

pinch of black pepper

8 ounces of diced vegetarian ham

4 cups hash browns (if using frozen, thaw first)

1 cup grated Gouda cheese

1 small yellow onion (diced)

1 red bell pepper (seeded and diced)

* 8 English muffins or biscuits to serve over

In a large mixing bowl, whisk together the eggs, 1/2 cup of milk and 1/4 teaspoon black pepper and set aside.

Melt the butter in a skillet over medium heat. Whisk in the flour until fully dissolved and turn off heat. Continue whisking continuously as you slowly pour in the 1/2 cup vegetable broth and 1/2 cup milk. Once mixture thickens, add in a pinch of sea salt and black pepper and transfer mixture into the bowl with the beaten egg mixture. Stir until all ingredients are well blended.

Combine the diced vegetarian ham, hash browns, grated Gouda, diced onion and bell pepper into your prepared slow cooker and give it a good stir to blend. Slowly pour the cream mixture over the ham mixture in your slow cooker WITHOUT stirring any further. Cook on "low" for 6-7 hours. Turn off heat, remove lid from slow cooker and let the finished breakfast bake rest for 15 minutes before serving over a warm English muffin or biscuit. Makes 8 servings.

Lemon Scone Breakfast Bread

Ingredients:

2 cups all-purpose flour

1 tablespoon aluminum-free baking powder

1/4 cup poppy seeds

1/2 teaspoon sea salt

3 large eggs

1 cup raw sugar

1/2 cup light oil (safflower, sunflower, grapeseed, etc.)

1/2 cup sour cream (regular or vegan)

1/4 cup plain milk (regular or non-dairy)

1/4 cup fresh squeezed lemon juice

1 teaspoon finely grated lemon peel

1 teaspoon pure vanilla extract

Grease the bottom and sides of your slow cooker with coconut oil or other light oil.

In a large mixing bowl, whisk together the flour, baking powder, poppy seeds and sea salt and set aside. In a separate mixing bowl, whisk the eggs until well beaten before stirring in all of the remaining ingredients. Pour the bowl with the wet ingredient mixture into the bowl with the dry ingredient mixture and stir just until all ingredients are moistened and evenly combined. Transfer batter into your prepared slow cooker. Cook on "high" for 2 hours, or until top looks set. Turn off slow cooker and carefully remove lid so that the condensation does not drip onto bread. Cover slow cooker with paper towels (this helps bread to set) and let stand for 15 minutes. Carefully run a knive around the edges to remove from slow cooker and transfer bread to a wire rack to fully cool before cutting and serving. Makes 8-10 servings.

Spinach and Mozzarella Breakfast Frittata

Ingredients:

2 tablespoons olive oil

1/2 cup diced onion

6 large eggs (well beaten)

2 tablespoons milk (regular or non-dairy)

1/2 teaspoon ground black pepper

1/4 teaspoon sea salt

1 large tomato (diced)

1 packed cup chopped fresh baby spinach

1 cup shredded Mozzarella cheese (divided)

*optional garnishes: salsa; sour cream; fresh chopped cilantro

Heat the olive oil in a skillet over medium heat. Add in the diced onions and saute until the onions become translucent, about 4 minutes. Add the sauteed onions into a mixing bowl, and stir in all of the remaining ingredients EXCEPT 1/4 cup of the shredded Mozzarella cheese. Stir until all ingredients are well combined.

Lightly oil the bottom and sides of your slow cooker. Pour in the frittata mixture and top with the remaining 1/4 cup of shredded cheese. Cook on "low" for 1-1/2 hours, or until knife comes out clean from the center. Serve with your favorite frittata garnishes (optional). Makes 4-6 servings.

Overnight Apricots and Cream Oatmeal

Ingredients:

1 cup steel cut oats (do not use instant oatmeal)

3 tablespoons packed brown sugar

1/2 teaspoon salt

1 cup dried apricots (finely chopped)

3 cups water

1-1/2 cups half-n-half

1 teaspoon pure vanilla extract

3 tablespoons wheat bran (optional)

*Optional oatmeal toppings: chopped dried apricots; finely chopped nuts; extra drizzle of half-n-half

Lightly oil the bottom and sides of your slow cooker with oil or butter. Combine all of the ingredients in a mixing bowl and stir until all ingredients are evenly coated and well combined. Pour mixture into your slow cooker and cook on "low" for 7-8 hours. Serve as-is, or with your favorite oatmeal toppings. Makes 3-5 servings.

Stacked Mexican Tortilla Breakfast Casserole

Ingredients:

1/4 cup diced green onions

1/4 cup fresh chopped cilantro

1/2 teaspoon sea salt

1/2 teaspoon ground cumin

3 tablespoons olive oil

5 large eggs (well beaten)

1 pound vegetarian sausage (diced)

1 green bell pepper (seeded and diced)

1 small jalapeno pepper (seeded and diced)

9 (6 inch size) corn tortillas

2 cups shredded Mexican cheese blend (divided)

1-1/2 cups salsa (divided - or more, as desired)

* fresh chopped cilantro and chopped black olives for garnish

Grease the bottom and sides of your slow cooker with oil.

In a large mixing bowl, stir together the green onions, 1/4 cup chopped cilantro, sea salt and ground cumin and set aside.

Heat the olive oil in a large skillet over medium heat. Add in the beaten eggs, diced vegetarian sausage, diced bell pepper and diced jalapeno pepper and cook while stirring frequently until eggs are cooked and all ingredients are well combined. Remove from heat and transfer egg mixture into bowl with seasoned green onion mixture and toss to evenly combine.

To assemble the casserole layer 3 of the corn tortillas into the bottom of your prepared slow cooker. Spoon half of the egg-sausage mixture across the top, followed by half of the shredded cheese and half of the salsa (2/3 cup). Repeat another layer of 3 corn tortillas, the remaining egg-sausage mixture, the remaining salsa and top with the last 3 corn tortillas. You can drizzle on a little extra salsa across the top of the assembled casserole. Cover and cook on "low" for 3-4 hours. Turn off heat, remove lid from slow cooker and let the casserole sit for 15 minutes before cutting and serving with a sprinkle of fresh chopped cilantro and black olives. Makes 6 servings.

Pumpkin and Berry Breakfast Bread

Ingredients:

3/4 cup pumpkin puree

1/2 cup half-and-half

2 tablespoons packed brown sugar

2 cups all-purpose flour

2 teaspoons aluminum-free baking powder

1-1/2 teaspoons pumpkin pie spice

1/2 teaspoon sea salt

4 tablespoons cold butter (cut into small pieces)

3/4 cup chopped fresh berries (blueberries, raspberries, cherries)

1 tablespoon all-purpose flour

1/2 cup pure maple syrup

2 tablespoons melted butter

1/2 cup finely chopped nuts (pecans or walnuts)

Liberally grease the bottom and sides of your slow cooker with butter OR you can also use a slow cooker liner.

Whisk together the pumpkin puree, half-and-half and brown sugar in a mixing bowl and set aside.

In a separate mixing bowl, whisk together the 2 cups of flour, baking powder, pumpkin pie spice and sea salt until well combined. Using a fork or pastry cutter, "cut" in the 4 tablespoons of cold butter until pieces look like wet sand. Add the pumpkin puree mixture into the bowl with the bowl with the flour mixture and stir very thoroughly to combine. In a small mixing bowl, toss together the chopped fresh berries and 1 tablespoon of flour until berries are evenly coated and stir them into the bowl with the other ingredients.

Transfer mixture into your prepared slow cooker and evenly drizzle the maple syrup, 2 tablespoons of melted butter and chopped nuts across the tops WITHOUT stirring mixture any further. Cook on "high" for 2-1/2 hours. Turn off slow cooker and carefully remove lid so that the condensation from lid does not drip onto bread. Cover the slow cooker with paper towels (this helps to set the bread) and allow bread to cool for 45-60 minutes before cutting and serving. Makes 6-8 servings.

Southwestern Veggie Omelet and Potato Bake

Ingredients:

3 tablespoons olive oil

1 yellow onion (diced)

1 large red bell pepper (seeded and diced)

2 fresh garlic cloves (minced)

12 large eggs (well beaten)

1/2 cup heavy cream

1-1/4 cup shredded Mexican cheese blend

1 bag (16 ounce) hash brown potatoes

1 teaspoon sea salt

1 teaspoon ground black pepper

1/2 teaspoon chili powder

* fresh chopped cilantro and black olives for garnish

Grease the bottom and sides of your slow cooker with butter or oil.

Heat the olive oil in a skillet over medium heat. Add in the diced onions and red bell peppers and saute until onions become translucent, about 4 minutes. Add in the minced garlic and stir continuously until fragrant, about 30-60 seconds. Transfer the sauteed mixture into a large mixing bowl along with the beaten eggs, half-and-half and shredded cheese and stir until combined. Stir in the hash brown potatoes and seasonings and transfer mixture into your prepared slow cooker. Cook on "low" for 6-8 hours. Serve with a sprinkle of fresh chopped cilantro and black olives. Makes 6 servings.

Design Your Own Mock Sausage Quiche

Ingredients:

1 dozen large eggs (well beaten)

1/2 cup melted butter

1/2 cup all-purpose flour

1 teaspoon aluminum-free baking powder

2 cups of chopped, cooked vegan sausage (you could also use vegan kielbasa)

2 cups cottage cheese

1-1/2 cups shredded Sharp Cheddar cheese

1-1/2 cups shredded Swiss cheese

1/2 teaspoon dried oregano

1/2 teaspoon dried thyme

1/2 teaspoon ground black pepper

1/2 teaspoon sea salt

*Optional quiche add-ins:

1 whole jalapeno pepper (seeded and diced)

3/4 cup diced yellow onion

1-1/2 cups diced mushrooms (any variety)

2-3 fresh garlic cloves (minced)

Using butter or oil, grease the bottom and sides of your slow cooker. In a large mixing bowl, whisk together the eggs, melted butter, flour and baking powder. Stir in all of the remaining ingredients, along with any, some or all of the suggested quiche add-ins, until all ingredients are evenly combined. Pour mixture into your prepared slow cooker and cook on "low" for 3-4 hours. Turn off heat and let the quiche set for 15 minutes before cutting and serving. Makes 4-6 servings.

Overnight Pear and Nut Oatmeal

Ingredients:

1 cup steel-cuts oats (do not use instant oatmeal)

4 cups non-dairy milk

2 large pears (peeled and diced)

1/4 teaspoon ground nutmeg

1 teaspoon pure vanilla extract

1 tablespoon pure maple syrup

2-3 tablespoons raw honey (do not use commercially processed honey)

1/2 heaping cup of finely chopped nuts (walnuts or pecans)

Lightly oil the bottom and sides of your slow cooker. Combine all of the ingredients in your slow cooker EXCEPT the crushed nuts. Stir well to blend and cook on "low" for 7-9 hours (great to do overnight, while you sleep). In the morning, stir the oatmeal well before serving. Serve with a sprinkling of the chopped nuts and any added natural sweetener (pure maple syrup, raw honey, stevia), if desired. Makes 4-6 servings.

Vegetarian Ham, Brie and Focaccia Brunch Bake

Ingredients:

4 large eggs (well beaten)

3 cups half-and-half

3 fresh garlic cloves (minced)

1 teaspoon dried thyme

1/4 teaspoon ground black pepper

6 cups of STALE, cube focaccia bread

1-1/2 cups diced vegan ham (you may also use a vegetarian kielbasa)

4 ounces Brie cheese (cut into dices)

1/3 cup sun-dried tomatoes (use the kind you buy in a pouch, NOT oil packed)

Grease the bottom and sides of your slow cooker with olive oil.

In a large mixing bowl, whisk together the eggs, half-and-half, minced garlic, thyme and black pepper. Add in all of the remaining ingredients and toss well to evenly coat and combine all ingredients. Transfer mixture into your prepared slow cooker. Cook on "low" for 4 hours, or until knife comes out clean from center. Mixture should "puff" during cooking time. Turn off heat and let stand for 30 minutes before serving. The center will deflate slightly while cooling. Makes 4-6 servings.

Southern Green Chile and Jalapeno Grits

Ingredients:

6 cups water

2 cups long-cooking grits (do NOT use quick-cooking or instant)

2 green chiles (seeded and finely diced)

1 jalapeno pepper (seeded and finely diced)

1/2 teaspoon paprika (regular or smoked)

1/2 teaspoon sea salt

pinch of cayenne powder

Combine all of the ingredients in your slow cooker. Stir well to blend and cook on "low" for 6-8 hours (good to do overnight) or on "high" for 2-3 hours. Stir well before serving, and serve with cooling or sweet toppings to offset the heat, such as butter, pure maple syrup, raw honey, shredded cheese, sour cream, etc. Makes 6-8 servings.

*NOTE: If you do decide to cook the grits on "high", the grits will tend to get a bit thick during cooking time, so add in an extra 1/4-1/2 cup of water.

French Toast Souffle

Ingredients:

1 loaf of sliced bread (slightly old bread works best, and preferably French or Sourdough)

12 large eggs

2 cups milk (regular or non-dairy)

2 tablespoons brown sugar

2 teaspoons pure vanilla extract

2 teaspoons ground cinnamon

pinch of sea salt

* your favorite French toast toppings such as real maple syrup, powdered sugar, applesauce, etc.

In a large, shallow bowl whisk the eggs until well beaten. Next, whisk in the milk, brown sugar, vanilla extract, ground cinnamon and sea salt until well blended. Dip each of the bread slices into the mixture, making sure both sides get evenly coated and arrange the dipped bread in layers into your slow cooker. Once you have dipped and layered all of the bread slices, drizzle the remainder of the mixture across the top. Cook on "low" for 6-8 hours. Remove lid from slow cooker during the last 20 or so minutes of cooking, this will allow the bread to toast and brown. Serve in carved scoops with real maple syrup, powdered sugar, applesauce or any other of your favorite French toast toppings. Makes about 8 servings. *Make sure to leave an inch or two of space at the top of your slow cooker, otherwise it will take longer to cook if your slow cooker is overfilled.

Overnight Cocoa and Coconut Oatmeal

Ingredients:

1 cup steel-cut oats (do NOT use instant-cooking oats)

4 cups coconut milk

2 tablespoons cocoa powder (unsweetened)

4 tablespoons finely shredded coconut (unsweetened)

2 teaspoons pure vanilla extract

1/2 teaspoon almond extract

pinch of sea salt

* chopped almonds and natural sweetener (raw honey, raw agave nectar, stevia) for topping

Coat the bottom and sides of your slow cooker with some coconut oil or butter. Combine all of the ingredients in your slow cooker. Stir well to blend and cook on "low" for 7-9 hours. Stir well and serve with sprinkle of chopped almonds and natural sweetener (optional). Makes 4-6 servings.

Mock Ham and Veggie Quiche

Ingredients:

5 tablespoons olive oil (divided)

1 large bunch of baby spinach (hand torn)

4 ounces of vegetarian ham (diced)

2 cups diced mushrooms (any variety)

1 red bell pepper (seeded and diced)

1-1/2 cups shredded Swiss cheese

8 large eggs (well beaten)

2 cups half-and-half

2 tablespoons diced green onion

1/2 teaspoon sea salt

1/2 teaspoon ground black pepper

1/2 teaspoon dried thyme

1/2 cup vegan biscuit mix (may also use Bisquick)

* fresh chopped parsley or chives for garnish

Liberally grease the bottom and sides of your slow cooker with butter or oil.

Heat 2 tablespoons of the olive oil in a large skillet over medium heat. Add in the hand torn baby spinach and minced garlic and stir continuously until spinach is wilted, about 1-2 minutes. Immediately transfer into a large mixing bowl. In the same skillet, heat the remaining 3 tablespoons of olive oil. Add in the diced vegetarian ham, mushrooms and bell pepper and stir frequently until vegetables become tender, about 4 minutes. Transfer sauteed mixture into the same bowl with the sauteed spinach, along with all of the remaining ingredient and stir very thoroughly until all ingredients are moistened and well combined. Transfer mixture into your prepared slow cooker and cook on "low" for 4-1/2 to 5 hours, or until knife comes out clean from center. Turn off heat and remove lid from slow cooker. Allow the quiche to sit for 15-20 minutes before cutting and serving with a sprinkle of fresh chopped parsley or chives. Makes 6-8 servings.

Caramel Pecan Hawaiian Sweet Bread Breakfast Bake

Ingredients:

4 cups milk (regular or non-dairy)

1/2 cup raw sugar (may also use coconut sugar)

1 tablespoon pure vanilla extract

1 teaspoon ground cinnamon

pinch of sea salt

9 cups of STALE, cubed Hawaiian sweet bread

1/2 cup of caramel ice-cream topping - PLUS more for topping

1/2 cup finely chopped pecans - PLUS more for topping (optional)

* warmed half-and-half or heavy cream for garnish (sweetened or unsweetened)

Grease the bottom and sides of your slow cooker with coconut oil.

In a large mixing bowl, whisk together the milk, raw sugar, vanilla extract, ground cinnamon and sea salt. Add in the stale, cubed Hawaiian bread and toss to evenly coat. Cover with plastic and let mixture stand for 20-30 minutes to allow the bread to absorb all the liquid. Once the bread has absorbed liquid stir in the 1/2 cup of caramel (heat slightly if necessary for ease of stirring) and 1/2 cup of chopped pecans. Transfer mixture into your prepared slow cooker and cook on "low" for 2-1/2 to 4-1/2 hours, or until knife comes out clean from center. (Hawaiian bread sets differently than French or sourdough bread, so cooking time may greatly vary and take longer. Be sure to keep close watch after the 2-1/2 hour mark.) Turn off slow cooker, remove lid and let stand for 30 minutes. Serve with a drizzle of extra caramel sauce and warmed half-and-half or cream. Makes 10-12 servings.

Layered Breakfast Brunch Bake

Ingredients:

1 package (16 ounces) frozen hash browns

8 ounces of diced vegan sausage or kielbasa (Field Roast, MorningStar, LightLife are all good brands)

1 small yellow onion (diced)

1 small bell pepper (any variety - seeded and diced)

3/4 cup shredded Sharp Cheddar cheese

6 large eggs (well beaten)

1/2 cup milk (regular or non-dairy)

1/2 teaspoon sea salt

1/2 teaspoon ground black pepper

Lightly oil the bottom and sides of your slow cooker. Arrange the hash browns in the bottom of your prepared slow cooker, followed by the diced vegan sausage and all of the remaining ingredients in the order that they are listed WITHOUT stirring. Cook on "low" for 8-9 hours. Turn off slow cooker and allow the breakfast brunch bake to rest for 10 minutes before cutting and serving. Makes 4 servings.

Banana Nut Bread Oatmeal

Ingredients:

1 cup steel cut oats (do not use instant or quick-cooking oats)

3 cups nut milk (may also use regular milk or other non-dairy milk)

1-1/3 cups water

2 large, ripe bananas

1 tablespoon pure vanilla extract

2 teaspoons ground cinnamon

1/4 cup chopped raisins

1/4 cup finely chopped nuts (walnuts or pecans)

Grease the bottom and sides of your slow cooker with butter.

Combine all of the ingredients EXCEPT the raisins and nuts in a blender and blend until nice and smooth. Transfer mixture into your prepared slow cooker and stir in the chopped raisins and nuts. Cook on "low" for 5-6 hours. You can cook this on "low" for up to 8 hours, but you'll need to add in an extra 1/4-1/3 cup almond milk to prevent burning. Makes 4 servings.

Apple Pie Sticky Breakfast Bread

Ingredients:

3/4 cup raw sugar

3/4 cup packed brown sugar

1 tablespoon ground cinnamon

1/4 teaspoon ground nutmeg

1/4 teaspoon ground ginger

tiny pinch of sea salt

4 cans (7 ounces each and 10 biscuits each) refrigerated biscuits (cut each biscuit into quarters)

1-1/2 cups peeled, diced red variety apples

1/2 cup finely chopped nuts (pecans or walnuts)

1/2 cup melted butter

1/3 cup apple juice

1 teaspoon pure vanilla extract

Liberally grease the bottom and sides of your slow cooker with butter.

In a mixing bowl, whisk together the raw sugar, brown sugar, cinnamon, nutmeg, ginger and sea salt. Once blended, sprinkle 2 tablespoons of the spiced sugar mixture evenly into the bottom of your prepared slow cooker. Add the quartered biscuit pieces, diced apples and chopped nuts into the bowl with the remaining spiced sugar mixture and toss well to evenly coat. Transfer the mixture into the slow cooker.

In a small mixing bowl whisk together the melted butter, apple juice and vanilla extract and drizzle evenly over the biscuit mixture in the slow cooker without stirring any further. Cook on "high" for 2-1/2 hours, or until toothpick or knife comes out clean from center. Turn off heat and carefully remove the slow cooker lid, making sure to not let the condensation drip onto the bread. Cover the slow cooker with paper towels (this helps the bread to set) and let stand for 15-30 minutes. Carefully run a knife around the edges to remove bread and transfer it to a serving plate, and let the bread cool for an additional 15 minutes before cutting and serving. Makes 12 servings.

Overnight Breakfast Casserole

Ingredients:

6 large eggs (well beaten)

1 heaping cup of diced vegetarian sausage of your choice

4 large potatoes (peeled and cubed)

1 cup milk (regular or non-dairy)

2 cups shredded Sharp Cheddar cheese

2 fresh garlic cloves (minced)

1/2 teaspoon sea salt

1/2 teaspoon ground black pepper

Grease the bottom and sides of your slow cooker with olive oil.

Combine all of the ingredients into a large mixing bowl and toss well to evenly coat and combine all ingredients. Transfer mixture into your prepared slow cooker. Cook on "low" for 6-8 hours.

Makes 4-6 servings. *I like to use Field Roast brand vegetarian sausages for this recipe, using either their Italian seasoned or Mexican Chipotle seasoned versions.

Sweet Chai Tea Breakfast Cake

Ingredients:

1/2 cup packed brown sugar

4 tablespoons butter

2 tablespoons chopped crystallized ginger

3 ripe pears (peeled and diced)

2 cups all-purpose flour

1 teaspoon baking soda

1 teaspoon ground cinnamon

1/2 teaspoon aluminum-free baking powder

1/4 teaspoon sea salt

1 stick of butter (softened to room temperature)

3/4 cup packed brown sugar

1 large egg

1/2 cup blackstrap molasses

1/2 cup fresh brewed chai tea (steep for at least 10 minutes before using - do NOT use bottled tea)

* powder sugar for garnish

Liberally grease the bottom and sides of your slow cooker with butter or coconut oil.

Combine the 1/2 cup packed brown sugar, 4 tablespoons of butter and chopped crystallized ginger in a saucepan over medium-low heat. Stir continuously until butter is fully melted and then stir in the diced pears. Transfer the sweetened pear mixture into your prepared slow cooker.

In a large mixing bowl, sift together the flour, baking soda, cinnamon, baking powder and sea salt. In a separate mixing bowl, beat together the softened butter, 3/4 cup packed brown sugar, egg and molasses until mixture is creamy and well blended. Pour half of the molasses mixture into the bowl with the dry flour mixture along with the fresh brewed chai tea and stir until well combined. Stir in the remaining molasses mixture and then transfer into your slow cooker on top of the sweetened pears WITHOUT stirring.

Place a cheesecloth (or clean kitchen towel) across the top of your slow cooker before placing on the lid. This will help absorb moisture so that the breakfast cake does not turn out soggy. Cook on "high" for 2 to 2-1/2 hours, or until toothpick comes out clean from center. Turn off heat and remove lid and towel. Let the cake rest for 15 minutes before carefully running a knife around the edges to loosen cake from sides of slow cooker. Place a flat plat or cutting board on top of slow cooker and carefully flip over to invert cake out of slow cooker. If cake sticks, you can just cut it into pieces directly in slow cooker. Serve with a dusting of powdered sugar. Makes 6-8 servings.

Stacked Challah Bread Vanilla and Almond French Toast

Ingredients:

1 loaf of STALE challah bread (sliced - may substitute with Hawaiian bread)

8 large eggs

2 cups heavy cream

2 cups plain milk (regular or non-dairy)

2 tablespoons raw sugar

2 teaspoons pure vanilla extract

1 teaspoon almond extract

1-1/2 teaspoons ground cinnamon

1/2 teaspoon sea salt

* French toast toppings: maple syrup; powdered sugar; fresh fruit; etc.

Grease the bottom and sides of your slow cooker with butter or coconut oil. Evenly layer the sliced, stale challah bread in your prepared slow cooker.

In a large mixing bowl, whisk the eggs until well beaten. Add in the remaining ingredients, one at a time, and whisk until mixture is well blended and then pour over the stacked challah bread. Let the mixture rest for 30 minutes while pushing down on it gently every 10 minutes to help the bread absorb the liquid mixture. After 30 minutes set your slow cooker to "low" and cook for 8 hours. Turn off slow cooker, remove lid and let stand for 15 minutes before cutting and serving with your favorite French toast toppings. Makes 6 servings.

Overnight Trail Mix Oatmeal

Ingredients:

1 cup steel cut oats

4 red variety apples (peeled and diced)

1 cup fresh cranberries (rough chopped)

1/4 cup raisins (dark or golden)

1/4 cup finely chopped nuts (walnuts or pecans)

1/2 teaspoon ground cinnamon

1/4 teaspoon ground nutmeg

1/8 teaspoon ground cloves

1/8 teaspoon ground ginger

pinch of sea salt

4 cups water

Lightly grease the bottom and sides of your slow cooker with butter or oil. Combine all of the ingredients into your slow cooker. Stir thoroughly to combine ingredients and cook on "low" for 8-9 hours. Serve with an optional drizzle of natural sweetener such as maple syrup, raw honey, raw agave nectar or stevia. Makes 4 servings.

Chapter 2 – Slow Cooker Recipes: Appetizers

Super Easy Spinach and Artichoke Dip

Ingredients:

1 jar (around 14 ounces) of artichoke hearts (liquid reserved, and well chopped)

1 large bunch of baby spinach (rough chop)

1/2 cup sour cream (regular or vegan)

1/2 cup mayo (regular or vegan - you may also substitute with 4 ounces of cream cheese, regular or vegan)

3 tablespoons finely minced jalapeno peppers (you may substitute with hot sauce or crushed red pepper flakes)

1 cup shredded Mozzarella cheese (divided)

1 cup shredded Parmesan cheese (divided)

pinch of ground black pepper

Combine all of the ingredients, using 1/2 cup of the Mozzarella cheese and 1/2 cup of the Parmesan cheese in a mixing bowl and stir until all ingredients are evenly coated and blended. Transfer mixture into your slow cooker and cook on "low" for 2 hours. After 2 hours, remove the lid and stir in the remaining 1/2 cup of Mozzarella cheese and 1/2 cup of Parmesan cheese and continue cooking on "low" with the lid removed until the cheese is fully melted. If the dip mixture becomes to thick or dry drizzle in some or all of the reserved artichoke heart liquid to reach desired consistency. Serve with your favorite crackers, cocktail bread, pita bread or chips, or veggie crudites. Makes approximately 6 servings as an appetizer.

Cheesy Beer Fondue

Ingredients:

1/2 of a yellow onion (very finely diced)

2 fresh garlic cloves (minced)

2 cups of grated extra sharp Cheddar cheese

1 cup of grated Gruyere cheese

1 tablespoon cornstarch (may also use arrowroot powder or tapioca starch)

1 teaspoon ground mustard powder

1 teaspoon caraway seeds (crush them with a rolling pin before adding)

12 ounces of beer

1/4 teaspoon sea salt

1/4 teaspoon ground black pepper

* optional add-ins for heat: hot sauce; crushed red pepper flakes

** suggested dipping foods; bread pieces, soft pretzels, crackers, baguettes and cut veggies

Combine all of the ingredients (and any optional add-ins, if using) into your slow cooker and stir very thoroughly to evenly blend and mix all ingredients. Cook on "low" for 2-4 hours, stirring every 20-30 minutes. If fondue becomes too thick, stir in a little extra beer. Taste and adjust seasonings as desired before serving with your favorite cheese fondue dipping foods.

Bean and Cheese Dip

Ingredients:

2 packages (8 ounces each) cream cheese (softened to room temperature)

2 cans (15 ounces each) refried beans (most are vegetarian, but check label to be sure)

3-4 green chiles (finely diced - or you can use one 4 ounce can of diced green chiles, drained)

1/4 cup finely diced onions

3/4 teaspoon garlic powder

1-1/2 cups shredded Cheddar cheese

hot sauce (to taste)

Combine all of the ingredients into your slow cooker EXCEPT the shredded cheese and hot sauce. Stir very thoroughly to blend and cook on "low" for 3 hours, stirring every 30 minutes or so. Stir in the shredded Cheese and hot sauce to taste during the last 30 minutes of cooking time. Taste and add sea salt and black pepper if desired before serving, but this is a naturally salty dish, so I don't recommend adding it beforehand. Serve with your favorite chips, crackers, cubed bread, baguettes or cut veggies.

Sweet and Spicy Meatballs

Ingredients:

2 bags (9 ounces each) vegetarian meatballs

3/4 cup apricot preserves

1/2 cup plain tomato sauce

2 tablespoons fresh squeezed lemon juice

1 tablespoon Braggs liquid aminos (may also use Tamari or regular soy sauce)

1 tablespoon fresh grated ginger root

1/8 teaspoon cayenne pepper

1/8 teaspoon ground black pepper

Combine all of the ingredients into your slow cooker. Stir well to blend and cook on "low" for 4-6 hours, stirring every 1-2 hours. Makes 6-8 servings as an appetizer.

Spicy Chile Cheese Dip

Ingredients:

3-4 tablespoons olive oil

1 yellow onion (diced)

6 green chiles (seeded and finely diced)

1 can (14 ounce) stewed Mexican tomatoes (with their liquid)

16 ounces of shredded Mexican cheese blend

Heat the olive oil in a skillet over medium heat. Add in the diced onions and green chiles and saute until onions become translucent, about 4-5 minutes. Transfer the sauteed mixture into your slow cooker along with all of the remaining ingredients. Stir well to blend and cook on "low" for 2 hours, stirring every 20-30 minutes. Serve with tortilla chips, bread cubes, baguettes or cut veggies.

Mock Pigs in a Bac'n Blanket Bites

Ingredients:

2 packages of veggie dogs (there are typically 5 to a package, so you'll have 10 veggie dogs)

3 packages of vegetarian bac'n strips

toothpicks

brown sugar

Cut each of the veggie dogs into 3 pieces each, so you'll have a total of 30 pieces. Cut each of the vegetarian bac'n pieces into halves (you may need to warm them slightly to make them more pliable and easy to work with), and wrap each half piece around one of the cut veggie dog pieces and secure with a toothpick. Once you have all of the pieces assembled, arrange a layer of the bac'n wrapped veggie dogs into the bottom of your slow cooker and liberally sprinkle with brown sugar. Repeat layering until all of the pieces are in the slow cooker and topped with a final liberal sprinkling of brown sugar. Cook on "low" for 4-6 hours. Makes 30 pieces.

Veggie Pizza Dip

Ingredients:

1 package (8 ounce) cream cheese (softened to room temperature)

1 jar (16-18 ounce) of marinara sauce

10 ounces of shredded Mozzarella cheese (or Italian cheese blend)

1/2 cup finely diced onion

1/2 cup finely diced green onion

1/2 cup finely diced black olive

1/2 cup finely diced mushrooms

3 fresh garlic cloves (minced)

1 teaspoon of Italian seasoning blend

In a mixing bowl, stir all of the ingredients together until evenly combined. Transfer mixture into your slow cooker and cook on "low" for 1-1/2 to 2 hours, stirring every 20-30 minutes. Serve with chips, crackers or cut veggies.

Marinated Mushrooms

Ingredients:

2 pounds of whole button mushrooms (stems removed)

2 cups Braggs liquid aminos (may substitute with Tamari)

2 cups water

2 sticks of butter (unsalted)

2 cups raw sugar

When prepping the mushrooms, if the mushrooms are on the small side, leave them whole after removing stems. If the mushrooms are on the larger side, then halve them.

Combine the Braggs liquid aminos (or Tamari sauce), water and butter in a saucepan over medium heat. Once the butter has melted, whisk in the raw sugar and continue whisking until fully dissolved. Combine the marinade mixture and mushrooms in your slow cooker and stir to blend. Cook on "low" for 8-9 hours, stirring every 1-2 hours if possible. Marinated mushrooms can be served either warm or cold. Makes about 10-12 servings as an appetizer.

Thick and Spicy Mock Beef and Cheese Dip

Ingredients:

3 tablespoons olive oil

1 large yellow onion (diced)

1 jalapeno pepper (seeded and diced)

2-3 green chile peppers (seeded and diced)

3-4 fresh garlic cloves (minced)

2 packages (12 ounces each) veggie crumbles

2-1/2 cups plain tomato sauce

2 teaspoons dried oregano

2 packages (8 ounces each) cream cheese (softened to room temperature and cut into cubes)

1/2 cup fresh grated Parmesan cheese

crushed red pepper flakes (to taste)

sea salt (to taste)

* tortilla chips to serve with dip

Heat the olive oil in a skillet over medium heat. Add in the diced onions and saute until onions become translucent, about 4 minutes. Add in the diced jalapeno pepper, green chili pepper and minced garlic, and stir continuously until fragrant, about 30-60 seconds. Transfer the sauteed mixture into your slow cooker along with all of the remaining ingredients. Stir very thoroughly to blend and cook on "low" for 3-4 hours, stirring every hour. If mixture becomes too thick during cooking time, add in a little extra tomato sauce (or water) to reach desired consistency. Taste and adjust seasonings as desired before serving with warm tortilla chips.

Caramel Rum Dip

Ingredients:

4 cups flavored baking chips (cinnamon, cappuccino, butterscotch or plain chocolate)

2/3 cup evaporated milk

2/3 cup finely chopped nuts (walnuts, pecans, macadamia, peanut)

2-3 tablespoons white rum

* fruit pieces or cake pieces on toothpicks for dipping

Stir together the butterscotch chips and evaporated milk in your slow cooker and cook on "low" for 1 hour. Stir in the chopped nuts and rum, and cook for another 15 minutes before serving.

Mock Barbecue Kielbasa Bites

Ingredients:

2 packages (12-14 ounces each) vegetarian kielbasa (cut into 1/4 inch round slices)

3/4 cup barbecue sauce

1/4 cup brown mustard

1/4 cup fresh orange juice

1/2 teaspoon fresh grated orange rind

Combine all of the ingredients into your slow cooker. Stir well to blend and cook on "low" for 4-6 hours, stirring every couple hours if possible. If mixture becomes too thick, add in a little extra orange juice to thin it out a bit. Makes 8 servings as an appetizer.

Spiked Caramel Fondue

Ingredients:

1 bag (14 ounce) plain caramels

2/3 cup heavy cream (will not turn out the same with regular milk or half-n-half)

1/2 cup mini marshmallows

1 tablespoon white rum

* fondue forks and fruit or cake pieces for dipping

Stir together the caramels and heavy cream in your slow cooker and cook on "low" for 1-1/2 to 2 hours, or until caramels are fully melted, stirring every 20-30 minutes. Stir in the mini marshmallows and rum and cook for an additional 30 minutes. Serve with fruit and/or cake pieces for dipping.

Chick'n Nachos

Ingredients:

2 bags (12 ounces each) vegetarian Chick'n strips (diced - I use LightLife brand)

2 cups corn

1 can (15 ounce) black beans (rinsed and drained)

2 cups medium or hot salsa

1 package (8 ounce) cream cheese (softened to room temperature)

1 can (15 ounce) black olives (drained and olives rough chopped)

* tortilla chips for serving nacho mixture over

Lightly grease the bottom and sides of your slow cooker with oil. Evenly layer the diced vegetarian chick'n pieces into the bottom of your prepared slow cooker, followed by the corn, black beans and salsa WITHOUT stirring. Cook on "low" for 2-4 hours, or until the chick'n pieces are thoroughly heated through. Stir in the softened cream cheese and chopped black olives and continue cooking until mixture is nice and creamy, about another 30 minutes. Serve mixture over warm or cold tortilla chips. Makes 6 servings as an appetizer.

Mediterranean Bean Dip

Ingredients:

1/4 cup olive oil

6 fresh garlic cloves (minced)

2 cans (15 ounces each) cannellini beans (rinsed and drained)

1/3 cup water

1 cup ricotta cheese

3/4 cup fresh grated Parmesan cheese

1 teaspoon dried rosemary

1/4 teaspoon ground black pepper

1/4 cup pitted kalamata olives (well chopped)

1/2 teaspoon fresh grated lemon peel

* fresh chopped rosemary for garnish

Heat the olive oil in a skillet over medium heat. Add in the minced garlic and stir continuously while sauteeing for 3 minutes. Reduce heat if necessary to prevent garlic from burning. Transfer the roasted garlic mixture into a blender or food processor along with all of the remaining ingredients EXCEPT the olives and lemon peel and puree until smooth. Transfer mixture into your slow cooker and cook on "low" for 1-1/2 to 2 hours, stirring every 30 minutes. Taste and adjust seasonings as desire and serve with a sprinkle of fresh chopped rosemary and your favorite crackers, chips or cut veggies.

Sweet and Spicy Mock Kielbasa Bites

Ingredients:

2 packages (14 ounce each) Tofurky kielbasa (sliced into 1/4-1/2 inch rounds)

1 jar (9 ounces) brown mustard (I use Eden brand organic brown mustard)

1 jar (18 ounces) apple jelly (regular, not the mint kind)

Toss together all of the ingredients in a mixing bowl until evenly coated and well blended. Transfer to your slow cooker and cook on "low" for 2 hours, stirring every 20-30 minutes. Makes 6-8 servings as an appetizer.

Spicy Artichoke Zucchini Spread

Ingredients:

2 jars (14 ounces each) artichoke hearts (drained and chopped)

2 medium sized zucchini (peeled and grated)

2 packages (8 ounces each) cream cheese (regular or vegan -

softened to room temperature)

2 cups sour cream (regular or vegan)

1/2 cup fresh grated Parmesan cheese

1 whole bunch of green onions (diced - green parts only)

2 teaspoons fresh squeezed lemon juice

1/2 teaspoon cayenne pepper

1/4 teaspoon ground black pepper

* hot sauce or crushed red pepper flakes (optional - for extra heat, if desired)

Lightly oil the bottom and sides of your slow cooker with oil.

Combine all of the ingredients into a large mixing bowl and stir very thoroughly until all ingredients are evenly blended. Transfer mixture into your prepared slow cooker and cook on "low" for 2-3 hours, stirring every 30 minutes. Serve with crackers, pita bread or veggies. Makes about 8-10 servings.

Pizza Fondue

Ingredients:

3-4 tablespoons olive oil

1 small yellow onion (diced)

2 cups diced mushrooms (any variety)

1/2 cup finely diced green bell pepper

3-4 fresh garlic cloves (minced)

1/2 cup chopped black olives

1 package (12 ounce) veggie crumbles

4 cups of your favorite marinara sauce

1 tablespoon Italian seasoning blend

sea salt and black pepper (to taste)

* fondue dippers: large diced sized pieces of mozzarella cheese; mini-sized cooked ravioli; cooked gnocchi; large hand torn pieces of French or Italian bread

Heat the olive oil in a skillet over medium heat. Add in the diced onions, mushrooms and green bell pepper and saute for 5 minutes. Add in the minced garlic and stir continuously until fragrant, about 30-60 seconds. Transfer the sauteed mixture into your slow cooker along with all of the remaining ingredients. Stir well to blend and cook on "low" for 3-4 hours. Serve with fondue forks and your favorite pizza fondue dippers. Makes approximately 5-6 cups worth of fondue.

Southwestern Style Spinach Dip

Ingredients:

2-3 tablespoons olive oil

2 bunches of baby spinach (hand torn)

2 packages (8 ounces each) cream cheese (softened to room temperature and cut into cubes)

1 pound of shredded Colby cheese

2-1/2 cups diced tomatoes

4 green chile peppers (seeded and diced)

2 fresh garlic cloves (minced)

1/4 teaspoon paprika

Grease the bottom and sides of your slow cooker with oil.

Heat the olive oil in a large skillet over medium heat. Add in the hand torn baby spinach and stir continously while sauteeing, until spinach is wilted. Immediately remove from heat and transfer into your slow cooker along with all of the remaining ingredients. Stir very thoroughly to blend and cook on "low" for 1-1/2 to 2 hours, stirring every 30 minutes. Makes about 8 servings.

German Style Kielbasa Bites

Ingredients:

2 packages (14 ounces each) vegetarian kielbasa (cut into 1/4 inch round slices)

1-1/4 cup applesauce (no sugar added)

3/4 cup packed brown sugar

2-3 tablespoons brown mustard

2 fresh garlic cloves (minced)

Combine all of the ingredients into your slow cooker. Stir to blend and cook on "low" for 4-6 hours, stirring every couple of hours if possible. Makes 8-10 servings as appetizers.

Party Favorite Vegetarian Cocktail Meatballs

Ingredients:

3 packages (9 ounces each) vegetarian meatballs

1-1/2 cups plain barbecue sauce

3/4 cup cranberry orange sauce (I use Indian Trail brand - found in cooler of produce department)

3/4 teaspoon ground ginger

3/4 teaspoon ground mustard

1/2 teaspoon sea salt

* fresh chopped parsley for garnish

Combine all of the ingredients into your slow cooker. Stir well to blend and cook on "low" for 3-4 hours, stirring every hour. Just before serving, sprinkle with some fresh chopped parsley (to taste) and give everything a good, gentle stir. Makes 12-16 servings as an appetizer.

Tex Mex Corn Dip

Ingredients:

2 packages (8 ounces each) cream cheese (softened to room temperature and cut into cubes)

2 sticks butter (unsalted - softened to room temperature)

3 cups corn

2 cups diced tomatoes

1 jalapeno pepper (seeded and diced)

1/2 of a large red or green bell pepper (seeded and diced)

1-2 fresh garlic cloves (minced)

crushed red pepper flakes (to taste)

Combine all of the ingredients into your slow cooker. Stir very thoroughly to blend and cook on "low" for about 1-1/2 to 2 hours. Makes about 6-7 cups of dip.

Chapter 3 –
Slow Cooker Recipes: Soups

Minestrone Soup

Ingredients:

6 cups vegetable broth

1 can (15 ounce) any variety of white bean (with liquid)

1/2 cup pearled barley (dry measurement)

2 cups diced tomatoes

1 medium zucchini (peeled and diced)

2 large yellow onions (diced or rough chopped)

3 large carrots (diced)

3-4 celery stalks (diced)

5-6 fresh garlic cloves (minced)

1 heaping handful of rough chopped kale (stems and ribs removed)

1-1/2 tablespoons dried parsley

1-1/2 teaspoons dried oregano

1 teaspoon dried thyme

1-1/4 teaspoons sea salt

1/2 teaspoon black pepper

1 cup of freshly grated cheese of choice for topping (Parmesan, Romano, etc.)

Combine all of the ingredients (except for the grated cheese) in a large slow cooker, cover and cook on "low" setting for 6-7 hours, or until vegetables are tender. Adjust seasonings as desired, and serve soup topped with the freshly grated cheese of your choice (optional). Makes 6-8 servings.

Veggie and Green Lentil Soup

Ingredients:

64 ounces vegetable broth

1 pound green lentils (soaked overnight and rinsed)

2 cups diced tomatoes

6 large celery stalks (diced)

4 large carrots (diced)

1 large yellow onion (rough chopped)

8 fresh garlic cloves (minced)

2 teaspoons dried oregano

2 teaspoons dried thyme

2-3 bay leaves

1 generous pinch of cayenne powder (or, to taste)

sea salt and black pepper (to taste)

1 large bunch of baby spinach (hand torn)

fresh lemon wedges

Combine all of the ingredients (except for the baby spinach and lemon wedges) in a large slow cooker and cook on "low" for 8-9 hours, or until lentils are fully cooked and soup has thickened. 5 minutes before you are ready to serve, adjust seasonings as desired and stir in the hand torn baby spinach. Cook just until the spinach has wilted. Remove bay leaves, ladle soup into individual serving bowls and serve each with a fresh lemon wedge to squeeze into soup before eating. Makes 8 servings.

Creamy Mushroom Soup

Ingredients:

2-3 tablespoons butter (regular or vegan)

3 heaping cups sliced mushrooms (any variety)

1 large onion (diced or rough chopped)

5 fresh garlic cloves (minced)

6 cups vegetable broth

4 tablespoons all-purpose flour

2 cups sour cream (regular or vegan)

2 cups milk (regular or non-dairy)

sea salt and black pepper (to taste)

Melt the butter in a large skillet over medium heat. Once melted, add in the sliced mushrooms, onions and garlic and sauté until onions becomes translucent, about 4-5 minutes. Stir frequently to prevent garlic from burning.

Add the sautéed mushroom mixture into a large slow cooker along with the vegetable broth and cook on "low" for 6-8 hours. Add in all of the remaining ingredients, stir well to fully dissolve the flour and cook on "high" for a final 30 minutes, or until soup thickens. Makes 6-8 servings.

Velvety Spiced Pumpkin Soup

Ingredients:

4 cups vegetable broth

16 ounces of pumpkin puree (canned or fresh)

1 cup finely diced celery

½ heaping cup thinly sliced carrots

½ heaping cup diced yellow onions

¾ teaspoon sea salt

½ teaspoon dried rosemary

½ teaspoon dried oregano

¼ teaspoon crushed red pepper flakes (or more, to taste)

2 large, firm tomatoes (diced)

raw or roasted pumpkin seeds (for garnish – optional)

Combine all of the ingredients, except for the diced tomatoes and pumpkin seeds, in a slow cooker and cook on "low" for 6-7 hours. During the final 30 minutes of cooking, stir in the diced tomatoes, and adjust any seasoning as desired. Ladle soup into individual serving bowls and garnish each with some of the raw or roasted pumpkin seeds, optional. Makes 4-6 servings.

Layered Split Pea Soup

Ingredients:

1 pound bag (16 ounces) of green split peas

4 large carrots (peeled and thinly sliced)

1-1/2 cups rough diced white or yellow onion

4-6 fresh garlic cloves (minced and then mashed into a paste)

1 large bay leaf

1 tablespoon sea salt

1 teaspoon black pepper

6 cups of hot (but not boiling) water

Rinse and drain the split peas, and then arrange them in the bottom of a slow cooker. Without stirring, even layer each additional ingredient on top of the previous ingredient, and then slowly pour the hot water over the top. This will help to keep the split peas towards the bottom of the slow cooker. Cook on "low" for 8-10 hours. Remove bay leaf, adjust any seasonings as desired and serve. Makes 8 servings.

Hot and Sour Soup with Mushrooms

Ingredients:

2 packages extra-firm tofu (pressed, drained and cubed)

16 ounces of thinly sliced mushrooms (any variety)

a handful of shiitake mushrooms (thinly sliced)

2 cans (8 ounces each) bamboo shoots (drained and cut into thin straw strips)

6 fresh garlic cloves (minced)

8 cups (64 ounces) vegetable broth

4 tablespoons Braggs liquid aminos (may also use Tamari or regular soy sauce)

4 tablespoons rice wine vinegar

2 teaspoons sesame oil

1-2 teaspoons chili paste (or, to heat and taste preference)

4 tablespoons fresh grated ginger root (divided)

3 cups green peas (if using frozen, thaw first)

*fine diced green onions for garnish (optional)

Combine all of the ingredients EXCEPT 2 tablespoons of the fresh grated ginger root and the green peas in your slow cooker. Stir well to blend and cook on "low" for 6-8 hours. Stir in the remaining 2 tablespoons of grated ginger along with the green peas during the last 30 minutes of cooking time. Taste the soup before serving to see if you want to add in an extra drizzle of vinegar or chili paste. Serve with an optional garnish of fine diced green onions. Makes 8 servings.

Easy Potato Leek Soup

Ingredients:

5-6 cups of vegetable broth (you need enough to cover all the vegetables)

4 large golden russet potatoes (peeled and cubed)

2 large leeks (ends trimmed and thoroughly and thinly chopped)

3 large carrots (thinly sliced)

2-3 large celery stalks (thinly diced)

4-5 fresh garlic cloves (minced)

3/4 teaspoon sea salt

1/2 teaspoon ground black pepper

* fresh chopped parsley, for garnish (optional)

** fresh heavy cream, for garnish (optional)

Combine all of the ingredients in your slow cooker. Stir well to blend and cook on "low" for 6-7 hours. Once the soup is done cooking, using a stick immersion blender, puree the soup to desired consistency in the slow cooker. If you don't have an immersion blender, you can transfer the soup in BATCHES to a blender or food processor (do not transfer the whole amount at one time - and never fill your blender more than 3/4 of the way full), puree to desired consistency and then return to the slow cooker. Serve with an optional garnish of fresh chopped parsley and a drizzle of fresh heavy cream (regular or non-dairy). This soup serves well with warm bread, or even in hollowed out bread bowls. Makes 6-8 servings.

Barley and Veggie Soup

Ingredients:

2-3 tablespoons olive oil

1 yellow onion (diced)

4-5 fresh garlic cloves (minced)

1 large carrot (sliced into thin rounds)

2 large celery stalks (diced)

2 cups thinly sliced mushrooms (any variety)

1/2 cup long-cooking barley (dry measurement - do NOT use quick-cooking barley)

1 can (15 ounce) white OR red kidney beans (rinsed and drained)

2 cups diced tomatoes

5-1/2 cups vegetable broth

1 tablespoon Italian seasoning blend

1/2 teaspoon ground black pepper

1/2 teaspoon sea salt

*fresh chopped parsley for garnish (optional)

Heat the olive oil in a skillet over medium heat. Add in the diced onions and saute until onions become translucent, about 4 minutes. Add in the minced garlic, sliced carrots, diced celery and sliced mushrooms and stir continuously while cooking for an additional 4-5 minutes. Transfer the sauteed vegetable mixture into your slow cooker along with all of the remaining ingredients. Stir well to blend and cook on "low" for 8-10 hours. Serve with a garnish of fresh chopped parsley (optional). Makes 4-6 servings.

Mexican-Style Minestrone

Ingredients:

6 cups (40 ounces) vegetable broth

3 cups diced tomatoes

1-1/2 cups corn

2 cups diced green beans

2 cups diced baby red potatoes

2 cans (15 ounces each) black beans (rinsed and drained)

1 can (15 ounce) chickpeas (rinsed and drained)

1 cup of your favorite salsa (I recommend a medium heat)

1 teaspoon sea salt

1 teaspoon ground black pepper

1 teaspoon ground cumin

*fresh chopped cilantro for garnish

Combine all of the ingredients into your slow cooker. Stir well to blend and cook on "low" for 8-10 hours. If soup becomes too thick for your liking, add in some more vegetable broth. Serve each portion with a sprinkle of fresh chopped cilantro. Makes 10-12 servings.

Zesty Quinoa, Potato and Corn Chowder

Ingredients:

3-4 tablespoons olive oil

1 small jalapeno pepper (seeded and diced)

3-4 fresh garlic cloves (minced)

1/2 tablespoon fresh grated ginger root

1 large celery stalk (finely diced)

1/2 of a large red or green bell pepper (seeded and finely diced)

2 golden russet potatoes (peeled and finely diced)

1 cup finely diced green beans

3/4 cup quinoa (dry measurement)

4 cups vegetable broth

2 bay leaves

1 teaspoon paprika

1 teaspoon ground coriander

1/2 teaspoon dried oregano

1/2 teaspoon dried thyme

1/2 teaspoon ground black pepper

1/2 teaspoon sea salt

2 cups of corn

2 tablespoons finely diced green onions

*fresh chopped cilantro for garnish

Heat the olive oil in a skillet over medium heat. Add in diced jalapeno, minced garlic, grated ginger root and diced celery and stir continuously while cooking for 2-3 minutes. Add in the diced bell pepper, diced potatoes and diced green beans and continue stirring continuously while cooking for an additional 2-3 minutes. Transfer the sauteed vegetable mixture into your slow cooker along with all of the remaining ingredients EXCEPT the corn and green onions. Stir well to blend and cook on "low" for about 6 hours. Stir in the corn and cook for another 30 minutes.

Before serving, remove the bay leaves and adjust seasonings as desire. Stir in the diced green onions and serve with a garnish of some fresh chopped cilantro. Makes 6 servings. *If you'd like to add an element of "heat" to the chowder, add in 1/8-1/2 teaspoon of cayenne powder or chili powder during cooking time.

Jamaican Soup

Ingredients:

2 tablespoons olive oil

1 small yellow onion (diced)

4 fresh garlic cloves (minced)

2 cups thinly sliced carrots

2 cups vegetable broth

1-1/2 cups coconut milk (unsweetened)

2 cans (15 ounces each) red kidney beans (rinsed and drained)

1-1/2 cups diced tomatoes

1 sweet potato (peeled and cubed)

2 teaspoons curry powder

1/2 teaspoon dried thyme

1/4-1/2 teaspoon crushed red pepper flakes

1/2 teaspoon sea salt

1/4 teaspoon ground black pepper

1/4 teaspoon ground allspice

*fresh chopped parsley or cilantro, for garnish (optional)

Heat the olive oil in a skillet over medium heat. Add in the diced onion and saute until onion becomes translucent, about 4 minutes. Add in the minced garlic and stir continuously until fragrant, about 30-60 seconds. Add the onion-garlic saute mixture into your slow cooker along with all of the remaining ingredients. Stir well to blend and cook on "low" for 6-8 hours. Taste and adjust seasoning as desired before serving. Serve with a sprinkling of fresh chopped parsley or cilantro. Makes 6 servings.

Zesty Black Bean Soup

Ingredients:

1 pound black beans (dry measurement)

2 tablespoons olive oil

1 onion (any variety - diced)

2-3 fresh garlic cloves (minced)

1 jalapeno pepper (seeded and diced)

6 cups vegetable broth

1 tablespoon chili powder

1 teaspoon ground cumin

1 teaspoon ground black pepper

sea salt (to taste)

hot sauce (to taste)

* fresh chopped cilantro for garnish

** Suggested optional soup toppings: shredded Cheddar cheese; sour cream; fresh lime wedges; salsa

Soak the black beans overnight. The next morning, drain, rinse and drain again.

Heat the olive oil in a skillet over medium heat. Add in the diced onions and saute until translucent, about 4 minutes. Add in the minced garlic and diced jalapeno peppers and stir continuously until fragrant, about 30-60 seconds. Transfer the sauteed onion mixture into your slow cooker along with the pre-soaked, rinsed beans and all of the remaining ingredients. Stir well to blend and cook on "low" for about 10 hours. Stir well before serving and serve with any, some or all of the suggested soup toppings. Makes 6 servings.

Mexican Style Gumbo

Ingredients:

2-3 tablespoons olive oil

1 large yellow onion (diced)

4 fresh garlic cloves (minced)

1 cup Basmati rice (dry measurement)

2 cans (15 ounces each) red kidney beans (rinsed and drained)

3 cups diced tomatoes

1 cup corn

1 jalapeno pepper (seeded and diced)

1 large can (15 ounces) plain tomato sauce

2 tablespoons tomato paste

3 cups vegetable broth (or more, as needed)

1-2 chipotle peppers in adobo sauce (diced - do NOT use the whole can, otherwise gumbo will be too spicy to eat)

4 teaspoons dried oregano

1 teaspoon smoked paprika

1/2 teaspoon ground cinnamon

2 tablespoons pure maple syrup (may also use raw agave nectar)

2 large bay leaves

* fresh chopped cilantro for garnish

Heat the olive oil in a skillet over medium heat. Add in the diced onions and saute until onions become translucent, about 4 minutes. Add in the minced garlic and stir continuously until fragrant, about 30-60 seconds.

Transfer the onion-garlic mixture into your slow cooker along with all of the remaining ingredients. Stir well to blend and cook on "low" for 6-8 hours. If gumbo becomes too thick, add in some more vegetable broth or water. Remove bay leaves and serve with a sprinkle of fresh chopped cilantro. Makes 4 servings.

Lentil and Rice Soup

Ingredients:

2 tablespoons olive oil

1 yellow or white onion (diced)

3-4 fresh garlic cloves (minced)

1 cup thinly sliced carrots

1/2 cup thinly diced celery

5 cups vegetable broth (or more, as needed)

1 cup lentils (dry measurement)

1 cup long-grain brown rice (dry measurement)

1 tablespoon table blend seasoning

1-1/2 teaspoons sea salt

1 teaspoon ground black pepper

8 ounces of thinly sliced mushrooms

* fresh chopped parsley for garnish

Heat the olive oil in a skillet over medium heat. Add in the diced onions and saute until onions become translucent, about 4 minutes. Add in the minced garlic and stir continuously until fragrant, about 30-60 seconds. Add in the sliced carrots and celery and stir continuously while cooking for an additional 2-3 minutes.

Transfer the sauteed vegetable mixture into your slow cooker along with all of the remaining ingredients EXCEPT the sliced mushrooms. Stir well to blend and cook on "low" for 7-9 hours. Stir in the sliced mushrooms during the last 1-2 hours of cooking time. If soup becomes too thick, add in more vegetable broth or water to reach desired consistency. Taste and adjust seasonings as desired and serve with a sprinkling of fresh chopped parsley. Makes 6 servings.

Easy Garden Soup

Ingredients:

2-3 tablespoons olive oil

1 yellow onion (diced)

3-4 fresh garlic cloves (minced)

5 cups (40 ounces) vegetable broth

3-4 large celery stalks (diced)

8 ounces of thinly sliced mushrooms

2-1/2 cups diced tomatoes

2 cups green peas

1 tablespoon Italian seasoning blend (you may also use a Table seasoning blend)

2 large bay leaves

1-1/2 teaspoons sea salt

1 teaspoon black pepper

*fresh chopped parsley for garnish

Heat the olive oil in a skillet over medium heat. Add in the diced onions and saute until onions become translucent, about 4 minutes. Add in the minced garlic and stir continuously until fragrant, about 30-60 seconds.

Transfer the onion-garlic mixture into your slow cooker and add in all of the remaining ingredients EXCEPT for the peas. Cook on "low" for 6-8 hours. Stir in the peas during the last 1 hour of cooking time. Remove the bay leave, and taste and adjust seasonings as desired. Serve with a sprinkle of fresh chopped parsley. Makes 4-6 servings.

Black Beans and Rice Soup

Ingredients:

2-3 tablespoons olive oil

1 large onion (diced)

4-6 fresh garlic cloves (minced)

3 large carrots (thinly sliced)

2-3 large celery stalks (thinly diced)

4 cups (32 ounces) vegetable broth (or more, as needed)

2 cans (15 ounces each) black beans (rinsed and drained)

1-1/2 cups diced tomatoes

1/2 tablespoon dried basil

1/2 tablespoon dried oregano

1/2 teaspoon chili powder

1/2 teaspoon ground cumin

1/2 teaspoon sea salt

hot sauce (to taste and heat preference)

1-1/2 cups cooked rice (any variety)

* fresh chopped parsley or cilantro for garnish

Heat the olive oil in a skillet over medium heat. Add in the onions and saute until the onions become translucent, about 4 minutes. Add in the minced garlic and stir continuously until fragrant, about 30-60 seconds. Add in the sliced carrots and celery and continue to stir frequently while cooking for an additional 2-3 minutes.

Transfer the sauteed vegetable mixture into your slow cooker along with all of the remaining ingredients EXCEPT the cooked rice. Stir well to blend and cook on "low" for 6-8 hours. Stir in the cooked rice during the last 1 hours of cooking time. If soup becomes too thick, just add in a little extra vegetable broth or water during cooking time. Taste and adjust seasonings as desired and serve with a sprinkle of fresh chopped parsley or cilantro. Makes 4-6 servings.

Easy Navy Bean Soup

Ingredients:

1 pound (16 ounces) navy beans (dry measurement)

3 tablespoons olive oil

1 yellow or white onion (diced)

3-4 fresh garlic cloves (minced)

6 cups (48 ounces) vegetable broth (or more, as needed)

3 cups diced tomatoes

1-1/2 teaspoon sea salt

1 teaspoon paprika (regular or smoked)

1 teaspoon dried thyme

1 large bay leaf

1/4 teaspoon crushed red pepper flakes

* fresh chopped parsley for garnish

Soak the navy beans overnight. The next morning, drain, rinse and drain again.

Heat the olive oil in a skillet over medium heat. Add in the diced onions and saute until onions become translucent, about 4 minutes. Add in the minced garlic and stir continuously until fragrant, about 30-60 seconds. Add the sauteed onion-garlic mixture into your slow cooker along with the pre-soaked beans and all of the remaining ingredients. Stir well to blend and cook on "low" for 6 hours, or until beans are tender. If soup becomes too thick for your liking, add in more vegetable broth or water to reach desired consistency. Remove bay leaf and taste and adjust seasonings as desired. Serve with a sprinkle of fresh chopped parsley. Makes 6-8 servings.

Taco Soup

Ingredients:

3 tablespoons olive oil

1 large yellow onion (diced)

3 fresh garlic cloves (minced)

1 jalapeno pepper (seeded and diced - use more or less, to taste)

2 cans (15 ounces each) pinto beans (rinsed and drained)

2 cups diced tomatoes

2 cups corn

1 teaspoon sea salt

1 teaspoon chili powder

1/2 teaspoon ground cumin

1/2 teaspoon dried thyme

2 cups vegetable broth (or more as desired, to reach desired consistency)

* suggested soup toppings and garnish; fresh chopped cilantro; fresh lime wedges; shredded cheese; sour cream; pico de gallo; tortilla chips

Heat the olive oil in a skillet over medium heat. Add in the diced onions and saute until onions become translucent, about 4 minutes. Add in the minced garlic and stir continuously until fragrant, about 30-60 seconds. Transfer the sauteed onion-garlic mixture into your slow cooker along with all of the remaining ingredients. Stir well to blend and cook on "low" for 4-6 hours. If soup is too thick for your liking, add in more vegetable broth during cooking time, to reach desired consistency. Taste and adjust seasonings as desired before serving with your favorite soup toppings and garnishes. Makes 4-6 servings.

Mock Ham and Split Pea Soup

Ingredients:

1 pound (16 ounces) of split peas (dry measurement)

2 tablespoons olive oil

1 large yellow onion (diced)

2-3 fresh garlic cloves (minced)

2 large carrots (thinly sliced or diced)

2 large celery stalks (diced)

10 ounces of vegetarian ham (diced)

3-1/2 cups vegetable broth

1 teaspoon dried marjoram

2 large bay leaves

sea salt and black pepper (to taste)

* fresh chopped parsley or dill for garnish

Soak the split peas for 15 minutes and then drain, rinse and drain again.

Heat the olive oil in a skillet over medium heat. Add in the diced onion and saute until onion becomes translucent, about 4 minutes. Add in the minced garlic and stir continuously until fragrant, about 30-60 seconds. Transfer the sauteed mixture into your slow cooker along with the soaked, rinsed split peas and all of the remaining ingredients. Stir well to blend and cook on "low" for about 6 hours, or until peas are nice and tender. Remove bay leaves and taste and adjust seasonings as desired, turn off slow cooker and let the soup sit for 10 minutes before serving with a sprinkle of fresh chopped parsley or dill. Makes 6 servings.

Creamy Country Succotash Chowder

Ingredients:

2 cups corn

2 cups lima beans

1 can (15 ounce) cream-style corn (with liquid)

1 cup diced red bell pepper

1 cup diced yellow onions

4 ounces grated smoked Gouda cheese

2 teaspoons ground cumin

1 teaspoon smoked paprika

1 teaspoon ground black pepper

1/4 cup vegetable broth (or more, as needed)

1 small container (8 ounces) sour cream

* fresh chopped parsley for garnish

Combine all of the ingredients into your slow cooker. Stir very thoroughly to blend and cook on "low" for 6 hours, giving the chowder a good stir several times during cooking time. Stir in the sour cream during the last 30 minutes of cooking time. If chowder becomes too thick, add in some more vegetable broth to reach desired consistency. Taste and add sea salt and black pepper as desired before serving. Serve with a sprinkle of fresh chopped parsley. Makes 6 servings.

Chipotle and Citrus Black Bean Soup

Ingredients:

1 pound bag (16 ounces) black beans (dry measurement)

1-1/2 cups diced tomatoes

1 large red bell pepper (diced)

3-4 fresh garlic cloves (minced)

1 tablespoon ground cumin

1 teaspoon ground cinnamon

1 teaspoon allspice

1 teaspoon chipotle chili powder

juice from 1 large sweet orange

juice from 1 large lime

4 cups vegetable broth

* fresh chopped cilantro and fresh lime wedges for garnish

** optional extra toppings/garnishes; sour cream, tortilla chips; shredded cheese

Soak the black beans overnight. The next morning, drain, rinse and drain again. Combine the soaked beans along with all of the other ingredients into your slow cooker. Stir thoroughly until all of the ingredients are evenly blended and the spices are fully dissolved and cook on "low" for 8-10 hours, or until the beans are very soft. If soup becomes too thick during cooking time, add in some more vegetable broth to reach desired consistency. Taste and adjust seasoning as desired before serving with a sprinkle of fresh chopped cilantro and fresh lime wedges for garnish. Makes 6 servings.

Creamy Italian Tomato Basil Soup

Ingredients:

2 cups milk (regular or non-dairy)

4 tablespoons butter (regular or vegan)

1 can (6 ounces) tomato paste

2 tablespoons all-purpose flour

1 tablespoons Italian seasoning blend

2 teaspoons sea salt

1/4 teaspoon ground black pepper

10-12 FRESH basil leaves (rough chopped)

12 large, ripe tomatoes (diced)

* fresh chopped parsley or basil for garnish

In a large mixing bowl, whisk together all of the ingredients EXCEPT the basil leaves and diced tomatoes until well blended. Pour mixture into your slow cooker and stir in the chopped basil leaves and diced tomatoes. Stir well to blend and cook on "low" for 6-8 hours, stirring several times during cooking time. If you wish to thicken the soup more, whisk in a little more flour to reach desired thickness. If you wish to thin the soup more, whisk in a little more milk. Taste and adjust seasonings as desired. You can serve the soup a bit on the thick side, or you can use a stick immersion blender to puree to desired consistency. If you don't have a stick immersion blender, you can transfer the soup in a couple batches into a blender, puree to desired consistency and return to slow cooker. Serve with a sprinkle of fresh chopped parsley or basil. Makes 4-6 servings.

Hearty Mock Beef and Broccoli Soup

Ingredients:

2 packages (12 ounces each) veggie crumbles (I use MorningStar or LightLife Smart Ground)

3 cups chopped broccoli

1 heaping cup diced mushrooms (any variety)

1 cup diced carrots

1/2 cup diced celery

1/4 cup diced red bell pepper

4-1/2 cups tomato juice

3-4 fresh garlic cloves (minced)

1/2 teaspoon dried oregano

1/2 teaspoon dried thyme

1/2 teaspoon sea salt

1/2 teaspoon ground black pepper

* fresh chopped parsley for garnish

Combine all of the ingredients in your slow cooker. Stir very thoroughly to blend and cook on "low" for 6-8 hours. Stir every couple of hours, and if soup becomes too thick during cooking time add in a little extra tomato juice (or water) to reach desired consistency. Taste and adjust seasonings as desired and serve with a sprinkle of fresh chopped parsley. Makes 6-8 servings.

Creole Mock Kielbasa, Greens and Veggie Soup

Ingredients:

3 tablespoons olive oil

1 yellow onion (diced)

4 fresh garlic cloves (minced)

1 cup diced red bell pepper

1 cup diced mushrooms (any variety)

4-6 ounces diced mock kielbasa (I use Tofurky brand)

2-1/2 cups diced tomatoes

2 cans (15 ounces each) cannelini beans (rinsed and drained)

5 cups vegetable broth

1/2-3/4 teaspoon Creole seasoning blend

1/4 teaspoon dried oregano

sea salt and black pepper (to taste)

1 large handful of well chopped greens (spinach, kale, turnip greens, mustard greens)

Heat the olive oil in a skillet over medium heat. Add in the diced onion and saute until onions become translucent, about 4 minutes. Add in the minced garlic and stir continuously until fragrant, about 30-60 seconds. Add in the diced bell peppers, mushrooms and kielbasa and cook for another 2-3 minutes while stirring continuously.

Transfer the sauteed mixture into your slow cooker along with all of the remaining ingredeints EXCEPT the greens. Stir well to blend and cook on "low" for 6-8 hours. If adding in spinach as your greens of choice, stir in during the last 30 minutes of cooking time. If using kale, turnip greens or mustard greens as your greens of choice, stir in during the last 1 hour of cooking time. If soup becomes too thick, add in a little extra vegetable broth or water to reach desired consistency. Taste and adjust seasonings as desired before serving. Makes 6 servings.

Cheesy Cauliflower Soup

Ingredients:

1 large head of cauliflower (chopped into small florettes)

3 tablespoons olive oil

1 large yellow onion (diced)

3-4 fresh garlic cloves (minced)

1/2 cup diced red bell pepper

1 teaspoon of dried oregano

4 cups vegetable broth

2 cups heavy cream OR half-and-half cream

1/2 teaspoon Worcestershire sauce (regular or vegan)

1 cup shredded Sharp Cheddar cheese

sea salt and black pepper (to taste)

* finely diced green onions for garnish

Heat the olive oil in a skillet over medium heat. Add in the diced onion and saute until translucent, about 4 minutes. Add in the minced garlic and stir continuously until fragrant, about 30-60 seconds. Transfer the onion-garlic mixture into your slow cooker along with the cauliflower, bell pepper, dried oregano and vegetable broth. Stir well to blend and cook on "low" for 6-7 hours.

If you prefer a cream vs. chunkier soup consistency, at this time use a stick immersion blender to puree the soup to desired consistency. Or, you can transfer the soup in batches to a blender and puree to desired consistency and return to slow cooker. If you prefer a chunkier soup consistency, then just skip this step.

Next, stir in the half-and-half, Worcestershire sauce, shredded cheese and sea salt and black pepper to taste. Cover and cook on "high" until cheese is fully melted, about 20-30 minutes. Taste and adjust seasonings as desired and serve with a sprinkle of diced green onions. Makes 4-6 servings.

Easy Creamy Mushroom Soup

Ingredients:

4 tablespoons butter (regular or vegan)

1 pound (16 ounced) of diced mushrooms (any variety)

1/2 cup diced yellow onion

3-4 fresh garlic cloves (minced)

3 cups vegetable broth

3/4 teaspoon sea salt

1/2 teaspoon ground black pepper

1/2 teaspoon dried thyme

1 cup sour cream (regular or vegan)

1 cup half-and-half

2 tablespoons all-purpose flour

* fresh chopped parsley for garnish

Melt the butter in a large skillet over medium heat. Add in the diced mushrooms and onions and saute until they become tender, about 4 minutes. Add in the minced garlic and stir continuously until fragrant, about 30-60 seconds. Transfer the mushroom-onion-garlic mixture into your slow cooker along with the vegetable broth, sea salt, black pepper and thyme. Stir well to blend and cook on "low" for 5-7 hours. During the last 30 minutes of cooking time, stir in the sour cream, half-and-half and flour and turn heat to "high". Soup will begin to slightly thicken. If you prefer an even thicker soup, add in another 1-2 teaspoons of all-purpose flour to reach desired consistency. Taste and adjust seasonings as desired and serve with a sprinkle of fresh chopped parsley. Makes 4-6 servings.

Chapter 4 –
Slow Cooker Recipes: Stews

Eggplant, Tomato and Bean Stew

Ingredients:

3 cups vegetable broth

6 ounces tomato paste

1 medium sized eggplant (peeled and cubed)

2 heaping cups diced tomatoes

1-1/2 cups sliced carrots

1 cup diced celery

1 cup diced yellow onion

6 fresh garlic cloves (minced)

1 can (15 ounces) chickpeas (rinsed and drained)

½ of a can cannellini beans (rinsed and drained)

1 large bay leaf

½ teaspoon sea salt

½ teaspoon dried oregano

½ teaspoon dried basil

¼ teaspoon black pepper

¼ teaspoon crushed red pepper flakes

Add the vegetable broth and tomato paste in a slow cooker and whisk it a bit to blend. Add in all of the remaining ingredients, stir to blend and then cook on "low" for 7-8 hours. If stew becomes too thick for your liking, add in more vegetable broth for desired consistency. Remove bay leaf and serve. Makes 4-6 servings.

Easy Veggie Stew

Ingredients:

2 yellow onions (diced)

2 large tomatoes (diced)

1 bell pepper, any variety (diced)

3-4 fresh garlic cloves (minced)

1-1/3 cups vegetable broth

12 ounces sliced mushrooms (any variety)

1 cup sliced carrots

8 ounces tempeh (diced)

2 tablespoons dried paprika

1 tablespoon dried parsley

2 teaspoon dried dill

½ teaspoon caraway seed

½ teaspoon sea salt

¼ teaspoon ground black pepper

1 package (10 ounces) soft tofu

1 cup peas (if using frozen, thaw first)

Combine the diced onions, diced tomatoes, diced bell pepper, minced garlic and vegetable broth in a blender, and puree until relatively smooth. Transfer the pureed mixture into your slow cooker and add in all of the remaining ingredients, EXCEPT for the tofu and peas, stir to blend and cook on "low" for 8-10 hours. As it nears the end of the cooking time, add the tofu into a blender or food processor and puree until very smooth. Spoon the pureed tofu along with the peas into the slow cooker, stir to blend and cook for a final 30 minutes. Serve as-is, over poured over a bed of fresh steamed rice, noodles or potatoes. Makes 4 servings.

Basic Greek Stew

Ingredients:

18 ounces vegetable broth

2 cups cubed butternut squash (may substitute with potatoes)

2 cups sliced carrots

2 yellow onions (rough chopped)

1-1/2 cups diced tomatoes

1 cup diced zucchini

1 can (15 ounce) chickpeas (rinsed and drained)

4 fresh garlic cloves (minced)

1 teaspoon ground cumin

½ teaspoon sea salt

½ teaspoon allspice

½ teaspoon ground coriander

½ teaspoon ground black pepper

½ cup finely crumbled Feta cheese

* 3-4 cups of freshly cooked couscous to serve stew upon.

Combine all of the ingredients, EXCEPT for the Feta cheese, in a slow cooker, stir to blend and cook on "low" for 7-9 hours. When ready to serve, serve as-is or over a bed of fresh steamed couscous and top with some of the finely crumbled Feta cheese. Makes 4-6 servings.

African Yam and Bean Stew

Ingredients:

3 cups vegetable broth

2 pounds yams (peeled and cubed)

1 can (15 ounce) red kidney beans (with liquid)

2 large tomatoes (diced)

1 large yellow onion (diced)

2 large red bell peppers (diced)

4-5 fresh garlic cloves (minced)

2 tablespoons fresh grated ginger root

1-2 jalapeno peppers (seeded and diced)

½ teaspoon sea salt

½ teaspoon ground cumin

½ teaspoon ground coriander

¼ teaspoon ground cinnamon

¼ teaspoon ground black pepper

¼ cup creamy style, natural peanut butter (no added sugar – room temperature)

1/3 cup chopped roasted peanuts

8 fresh lime wedges

Combine all of the ingredients EXCEPT the peanut butter, peanuts and lime wedges in a slow cooker, stir to blend and cook on "low" for 8-10 hours. Add in the peanut butter during the last 30 minutes of cooking, stir to evenly blend. Ladle stew into individual serving bowls, top with a sprinkle of the chopped roasted peanuts and serve each portion with a fresh lime wedge to squeeze into the stew before eating. Makes 6-8 servings.

Barley Stew

Ingredients:

2 tablespoons miso paste

2 tablespoons olive oil

6 cups vegetable broth

1 heaping cup pearled barley

4 large golden russet potatoes (peeled and cubed)

1 can (15 ounces) any variety of white beans (with liquid)

1/3 cup fine diced celery

2 tablespoons finely diced green chilies

2 teaspoons sea salt

generous splash of dark beer (optional)

Whisk together the miso paste and olive oil in the bottom of your slow cooker until well blended. Once blended, add in all of the remaining ingredients, stir to blend and cook on "low" for 5-6 hours. Stew serves well with some warm Sourdough bread, French bread or Pita bread. Makes 4-6 servings.

Millet and Veggie Stew

Ingredients:

1 cup millet (dry measurement)

4 cups vegetable broth

2 large golden russet potatoes (peeled and cubed)

2 yellow onions (rough chopped)

2 large carrots (sliced)

1 cup diced celery

8 ounces thinly sliced mushrooms (any variety)

2 large bay leaves

½ teaspoon dried oregano

½ teaspoon dried basil

½ teaspoon dried thyme

½ teaspoon sea salt

½ teaspoon ground black pepper

Heat an ungreased skillet over medium-low heat (no higher). Once heated, add in the millet and cook until lightly toasted while shaking skillet frequently to prevent burning, about 4-5 minutes.

Add the toasted millet along with all of the remaining ingredients into your slow cooker and cook on "low" for 8 hours. Serve with an optional garnish of fresh chopped parsley. Makes 4-6 servings.

Moroccan Squash Stew

Ingredients:

1-1/2 cups vegetable broth

1 butternut squash (peeled and cubed)

1 yellow onion (diced)

1-1/2 cups diced tomatoes

2 large carrots (diced)

1 can (15 ounce) chickpeas (with liquid)

½ heaping cup of finely chopped pitted prunes

1 teaspoon ground cinnamon

½ teaspoon crushed red pepper flakes

½ teaspoon sea salt

½ teaspoon ground black pepper

3 tablespoons fresh chopped parsley or cilantro

3 cups of fresh cooked grains (couscous; quinoa; barley, etc)

Combine all of the ingredients EXCEPT for the 3 cups of fresh cooked grains and 3 tablespoons of fresh chopped parsley in your slow cooker, stir to blend and cook on "low" for 6-8 hours. Stir in the fresh chopped parsley during the last 15 minutes of cooking time. Adjust seasonings as desired, spoon the squash stew over a scoop of fresh cooked grains of your choice and serve. Makes 4-6 servings.

Potato and Black Eyed Pea Stew

Ingredients:

1 pound black-eyed peas (dry measurement)

2 pounds of golden russet potatoes (peeled and cubed)

2 yellow onions (diced)

2 large tomatoes OR 3 small tomatoes (diced)

2 cups vegetable broth or water (or more, as needed)

6 fresh garlic cloves (minced)

1 tablespoon smoked paprika

1 teaspoon chili powder

1/4 teaspoon ground cumin

1/4 teaspoon ground coriander

2 large bay leaves

1/4 teaspoon sea salt

1/4 teaspoon ground black pepper

2 cups of corn (if using frozen, thaw first - if using canned, drain first)

Put the black eyed peas in a large bowl or pot, cover with water and soak overnight. The next day, drain the beans, rinse and drain again.

Add the soaked black eyed peas along with all of the remaining ingredients EXCEPT the corn into your slow cooker, stir to blend and then cook on "low" for 7-8 hours. Stir in the 2 cups of corn during the last 30 minutes of cooking time. Remove bay leaves and serve as-is, or with some fresh baked cornbread or hot French bread. Makes 6 servings.

Nothing but Veggies Stew

Ingredients:

1 large eggplant (peeled and cubed)

sea salt

3 large zucchini (peeled and rough chopped or sliced)

2 yellow onions (diced)

3 large tomatoes (diced)

1 large green bell pepper (seeded and rough diced)

1 large red bell pepper (seeded and rough diced)

3-4 tablespoons olive oil

3 tablespoons dried basil

3-4 fresh garlic cloves (minced)

1/2 teaspoon sea salt

1/2 teaspoon ground black pepper

1 can (6 ounces) tomato paste

1 can (6 ounces) black olives (drained and chopped)

3 tablespoon fresh chopped basil

Sprinkle the cubed eggplant liberally with sea salt and place in a large colander in your sink or over a bowl or pan. Allow the eggplant to cure and drain for 1 hour. After 1 hour, gently push down on the eggplant to release any remaining moisture and pat dry with paper towels. *Do not skip this step. Eggplant has a high water content, and if you don't "cure" and press out the excess moisture your dish will turn out mushy.

Add your prepped eggplant along with all of the remaining ingredients EXCEPT the tomato paste, black olives and fresh chopped basil in your slow cooker. Stir to blend and cook on "low" for 6 hours, or until vegetables are tender but still hold their shape. During the last 30 minutes of cooking time, stir in the tomato paste and chopped black olives. Serve with a sprinkle of the fresh chopped basil as-is, or over a bed of fresh steamed rice, potatoes or grains such as quinoa or barley. Makes 6-8 servings.

Hearty Lentil and Veggie Stew

Ingredients:

1 pound lentils (dry measurement, any variety)

3 tablespoons olive oil

2 cups diced yellow onion

4-5 fresh garlic cloves (minced)

2 large celery stalks (diced)

2 large carrots (diced)

8 cups vegetable broth

1 large head of cauliflower (cut into small florets)

2 leeks (ends trimmed and both white and green parts chopped)

2 cups chopped kale

2-1/2 cups diced tomatoes

2 large bay leaves

2 teaspoons sea salt

1 teaspoon ground cumin

1 teaspoon dried thyme

1/4 teaspoon cayenne powder

1/4 teaspoon ground black pepper

Thoroughly rinse and drain the lentils and set aside.

Heat the olive oil in a skillet over medium heat. Once heated, add in the diced onion and saute until onions become translucent, about 4 minutes. Add in the minced garlic, diced celery and diced carrots and stir continuously while cooking for an additional 4-5 minutes.

Transfer the sauteed vegetable mixture into your slow cooker along with the rinsed lentils and all of the remaining ingredients. Stir well to blend. Cook on "low" for 8 hours. Remove the bay leaves and taste the stew to see if you need to adjust any seasonings to desired taste. Serve as-is or over a bed of fresh steamed rice. Suggested stew toppings include finely crumbled Feta cheese, grated Parmesan cheese or a dollop of Greek style yogurt. Makes 8 servings.

Curried Coconut Squash and Chickpea Stew

Ingredients:

1-1/2 cups chickpeas (dry measurement)

2 tablespoons olive oil

1 large yellow onion (diced)

3 fresh garlic cloves (minced)

3 cups (24 ounces) vegetable broth or water

1 can (14 ounces) coconut milk

2-1/2 cups peeled, cubed squash (may substitute with potatoes)

2-3 large tomatoes (diced)

3 tablespoons of your favorite curry powder

1-1/2 teaspoons sea salt

1 large bunch of baby spinach (hand torn)

1-1/2 cups green peas (if using frozen, thaw first)

* fresh chopped parsley for garnish (optional)

** fresh steamed rice for serving stew on top of (optional)

Soak the dry chickpeas for a minimum of 12 hours, preferably up to 24 hours before ready to use. Drain, rinse and drain again.

Combine the soaked chickpeas along with all of the remaining ingredients EXCEPT the baby spinach and green peas in your slow cooker. Stir well to blend and cook on "low" for 7-8 hours. Stir in the baby spinach and green peas during the last 30 minutes of cooking time. If the stew isn't as thick as you would like at the end of the cooking time, stir in a little cornstarch or flour (just a LITTLE), and keep stirring as the stew continues to thicken. Serve as-is, or over a bed of fresh steamed rice with an optional garnish of fresh chopped parsley. Makes 6-8 servings.

Zesty Southwest Style Bean and Quinoa Stew

Ingredients:

2 tablespoons olive oil

1 large red onion (diced)

4 fresh garlic cloves (minced)

2 bell peppers (any variety - seeded and diced)

7-1/2 cups (56 ounces) vegetable broth

1 pound of black beans (dry measurement)

3/4 cup quinoa (dry measurement)

2 cups diced tomatoes

2 whole, dried chipotle peppers

2 teaspoons chili powder

1 large cinnamon stick (keep whole)

1 teaspoon ground coriander

1/2 teaspoon sea salt

1/2 teaspoon ground black pepper

* optional garnishes: fresh chopped cilantro; fresh lime wedges; sour cream; salsa

Soak the black beans overnight. Drain, rinse and drain again.

Heat the olive oil in a skillet over medium heat. Add in the diced onion and saute for 4 minutes. Stir in the minced garlic and diced bell peppers and stir continuously while cooking for an additional 4 minutes.

Transfer the sauteed vegetables into your slow cooker, along with the soaked black beans and all of the remaining ingredients. Stir well to blend and cook on "low" for 7-8 hours, or until the beans are thoroughly cooked and tender. Remove the dried chipotle peppers and cinnamon stick and serve with any or some of the optional garnishes. Makes 6-8 servings.

Asian-Inspired Stew

Ingredients:

3 tablespoons olive oil

1 yellow onion (diced)

4 fresh garlic cloves (minced)

3 large carrots (sliced)

3 large golden russet potatoes (peeled and cubed)

1 cup vegetable broth (or more as needed)

1 cup tomato sauce

1/4 cup nut butter (peanut, almond or cashew)

2 tablespoons Braggs liquid aminos (may also use Tamari or

regular soy sauce)

2 teaspoons fresh grated ginger root

8 ounces seitan (diced)

* fine diced green onions for garnish

Heat the olive oil in a skillet over medium heat. Add in the diced onions and saute until translucent, about 4 minutes. Add in the minced garlic and stir continuously until fragrant, about 30-60 seconds. Add in the diced carrots and potatoes and stir frequently while cooking for an additional 3-4 minutes. Remove from heat.

Whisk together the vegetable broth, tomato sauce, nut butter, liquid aminos and grated ginger root in the bottom of your slow cooker until the nut butter thins out a bit. Add in the sauteed vegetable mixture and the diced seitan. Stir well to blend and cook on "low" for 6-8 hours. If stew becomes too thick during cooking time, add in some more vegetable broth to reach desired consistency. Sprinkle each serving with some of the diced green onions and serve as-is, or over a scoop of fresh steamed rice. Makes 4 servings.

Classic Veggie Stew

Ingredients:

2-3 tablespoons olive oil

1 large yellow onion (diced)

4 fresh garlic cloves (minced)

2 large celery stalks (diced)

3 large carrots (sliced)

1 cup sliced mushrooms

4 large golden russet potatoes (peeled and cubed)

1/2 cup corn

1/2 cup green peas

1/2 cup green beans

1/2 cup diced tomatoes

6 cups vegetable broth

2 tablespoons table Italian seasoning blend

2 large bay leaves

1 teaspoon sea salt

1/2 teaspoon ground black pepper

* all-purpose flour to thicken (if needed)

Heat the olive oil in a skillet over medium heat. Add in the diced onions and saute until onions become translucent, about 4 minutes. Add in the minced garlic and stir continuously until fragrant, about 30-60 seconds. Add in the diced celery, carrots and mushrooms and continue to stir frequently while cooking for an additional 3-4 minutes.

Transfer the sauteed vegetable mixture into your slow cooker along with all of the remaining ingredients. Stir well to blend and cook on "low" for 7-9 hours. Remove bay leaves. Taste the stew and adjust any seasonings as desired. If you wish to thicken up the stew a bit, stir in a little all-purpose flour. Serve as-is, or over a bed of fresh steamed rice or grains. Makes 4-6 servings.

Beans, Greens and Potato Stew

Ingredients:

2-3 tablespoons olive oil

1 yellow onion (diced)

4 fresh garlic cloves (minced)

1 large bell pepper, any variety (seeded and diced)

4 large golden russet potatoes (peeled and cubed)

1-1/2 cups diced tomatoes

2 cans (15 ounces each) white kidney beans (rinsed and drained)

2 cups of rough chopped greens (Kale, Collard Greens, Swiss Chard, Mustard Greens or Turnip Greens)

3-1/2 cups vegetable broth (or more, as needed)

2 tablespoons Italian seasoning blend (you may also use a basic Table seasoning blend)

1 teaspoon sea salt

1/2 teaspoon ground black pepper

2 large bay leaves

* fresh chopped parsley for garnish

Heat the olive oil in a skillet over medium heat. Add in the onions and saute until onions become translucent, about 4 minutes. Add in the minced garlic and stir continuously until fragrant, about 30-60 seconds. Transfer the onion-garlic saute into your slow cooker and add in all of the remaining ingredients. Stir well to blend and cook on "low" for 5-6 hours. Remove the bay leaves, and taste and adjust seasonings as desired. Serve as-is or over a scoop of fresh steamed rice or grains with a sprinkle of fresh chopped parsley. Makes 6 servings.

Italian Eggplant and Tomato Stew

Ingredients:

2-3 tablespoons olive oil

1 large onion (diced)

4-5 fresh garlic cloves (minced)

1-1/2 cups thinly sliced carrots

1 cup thinly diced celery

1 medium sized eggplant (peeled and cubed)

2 cups diced tomatoes

1 can (15 ounce) chickpeas (rinsed and drained)

1/2 of a can (8 ounces of a 15 ounce can) red kidney beans (rinsed and drained)

3 cups vegetable broth (or more, as needed)

1 can (6 ounces) tomato paste

1 tablespoon Italian seasoning blend

1-2 large bay leaves

1/2 teaspoon sea salt

1/2 teaspoon ground black pepper

* fresh chopped parsley for garnish

Heat the olive oil in a skillet over medium heat. Add in the onions and saute until the onions become translucent, about 4 minutes. Add in the minced garlic and stir continuously until fragrant, about 30-60 seconds. Add in the sliced carrots and celery and continue to stir frequently while cooking for another 2-3 minutes.

Transfer the sauteed vegetable mixture into your slow cooker along with the cubed eggplant, diced tomatoes, chickpeas and kidney beans. Stir well to blend. In a mixing bowl, whisk together the vegetable broth, tomato paste and seasonings until the tomato paste starts to thin and blend. Pour over the other ingredients and stir well to evenly blend. Cook on "low" for 6-8 hour. Remove bay leaves, and taste and adjust seasonings as desire. Serve with a sprinkle of fresh chopped parsley. Makes 6 servings.

Layered Potato and Veggie Stew

Ingredients:

4 tablespoons olive oil

1 whole and 1/2 of a yellow onion (diced)

5 fresh garlic cloves (minced)

8 large golden russet potatoes (peeled and cubed)

2 large carrots (thinly sliced)

2 large celery stalks (diced)

2 cups diced veggies of your choice (green beans, cauliflower, eggplant, corn, green peas, mushrooms, etc.)

2 cups diced tomatoes

1-1/2 cups tomato sauce

1 tablespoon Italian seasoning blend (you may also use a table seasoning blend)

2 large bay leaves

2 teaspoons sea salt

1 teaspoon ground black pepper

splash of balsamic vinegar

* vegetable broth or water (as needed, to keep desired consistency)

** fresh chopped parsley for garnish

Heat the olive oil in a skillet over medium heat. Add in the diced onion and saute until onions become translucent, about 4 minutes. Add in the minced garlic and stir continuously until fragrant, about 30-60 seconds. Brush a little bit of olive into the bottom of your slow cooker and then evenly spread the sauteed onion-garlic mixture on top.

Next, evenly layer the remaining ingredients into your slow cooker in the order they are listed WITHOUT stirring. Cook on "low" for 8 hours. Keep watch of the stew towards the last couple hours of cooking time. If it looks like it is getting too dry, then add in some vegetable broth or water to reach desired consistency. Remove bay leaves and give the stir a good stir to blend. Taste and adjust seasonings as desired before serving with a sprinkle of fresh chopped parsley. Makes 6-8 servings.

Veggie and Chickpea Stew

Ingredients:

3-4 tablespoons olive oil

1 large yellow onion (diced)

3-4 fresh garlic cloves (minced)

4 large carrots (thinly sliced)

2 large celery stalks (diced)

3 cups diced mushrooms (any variety)

1 cup diced tomatoes

1/2 cup diced sundried tomatoes

1-1/2 cans (1 whole 15 ounce and 1 half of a 15 ounce) chickpeas (rinsed and drained)

3 cups vegetable broth

1 teaspoon sea salt

1 teaspoon ground cumin

1 teaspoon dried thyme

1/4 teaspoon crushed red pepper flakes

1 zucchini (peeled and diced)

* fresh chopped parsley for garnish

Heat the olive oil in a skillet over medium heat. Add in the diced onions and saute until onions become translucent, about 4 minutes.

Add in the minced garlic and stir continuously until fragrant, about 30-60 seconds. Transfer the sauteed onion-garlic mixture into your slow cooker along with all of the remaining ingredients EXCEPT for the zucchini. Stir thoroughly to blend and cook on "low" for 6-8 hours. Stir in the diced zucchini during the last 1 hour of cooking time. Taste and adjust seasonings as desired before serving. Serve as-is, or over some fresh steamed rice with a sprinkle of fresh chopped parsley. Makes 6-8 servings.

Italian Eggplant and Zucchini Stew

Ingredients:

4-1/2 cups peeled, cubed eggplant

1-1/2 cups peeled, cubed zucchini

1-1/2 cups diced tomatoes

1 cup diced bell pepper (any variety)

1 cup diced onion

4 fresh garlic cloves (minced)

1-1/2 cups tomato sauce (or more, as needed)

1 tablespoon Italian seasoning blend

1 teaspoon sea salt

1 teaspoon ground black pepper

1-2 large bay leaves

* fresh grated parmesan cheese and fresh chopped parsley for garnish

Combine all of the ingredients into your slow cooker. Stir well to blend and cook on "low" for 5-6 hours. Remove bay leaves and taste and adjust seasonings as desired. If stew becomes too thick during cooking time, add in a little more tomato sauce to reach desired consistency. Serve as-is, or over fresh steamed rice topped with fresh grated parmesan cheese and fresh chopped parsley. Makes 6 servings.

Hearty Winter Stew

Ingredients:

4 tablespoons olive oil

2 yellow onions (diced)

6 carrots (thinly sliced)

6 celery stalks (diced)

5-6 fresh garlic cloves (minced)

1 tablespoon tomato paste

1/4 cup balsamic vinegar

1 tablespoon brown mustard

2 cups lentils (rinsed and drained well before using)

2 golden russet potatoes (peeled and cubed)

4 cups vegetable broth

2-3 teaspoons dried thyme

1 teaspoon sea salt

1 teaspoon ground black pepper

1 pound bunch of fresh baby spinach (hand torn)

Heat the olive oil in a skillet over medium heat. Add in the diced onions, carrots and celery and saute until onions become translucent, about 4 minutes. Add in the minced garlic and stir continuously until fragrant, about 30-60 seconds. Stir in the tomato paste, balsamic vinegar and mustard and cook for an additional 1 minute. Transfer the sauteed mixture into your slow cooker along with all of the remaining ingredients EXCEPT the spinach. Stir very thoroughly to blend and cook on "low" for 8-9 hours. Stir in the hand torn baby spinach during the last 30 minutes of cooking. If stew becomes too thick, add in more vegetable broth to reach desired consistency. Taste and adjust seasonings as desired and serve as-is or over fresh steamed rice for a hearty, warming meal. Makes 6-8 servings.

Gypsy Stew

Ingredients:

1/4 cup olive oil

1-1/4 teaspoons ground ginger

1/2 teaspoon ground coriander

1/4 teaspoon sea salt

1/4 teaspoon ground cumin

1/8 teaspoon cayenne pepper

1/8 teaspoon ground turmeric

1/8 teaspoon ground black pepper

2 yellow onions (diced)

6 large golden russet potatoes (peeled and cubed)

4 parsnips (peeled and cubed)

4 large carrots (peeled and thinly sliced)

1 can (15 ounce) chickpeas (rinsed and drained)

3 cups vegetable broth (or more, as needed)

1/2-1/3 cup golden raisins

1-1/2 tablespoons apple cider vinegar

1 cinnamon stick

1 large bunch of fresh baby spinach (hand torn)

* fresh chopped parsley for garnish

In a mixing bowl, whisk together the olive oil and all of the spices until well blended. Heat the spiced olive oil in a skillet over medium-low heat (no higher, otherwise the spices will burn). Add in the diced onions and cook until onions become tender and translucent, about 7 minutes. Transfer the sauteed mixture into your slow cooker along with all of the remaining ingredients EXCEPT the baby spinach. Stir very thoroughly to blend and cook on "low" for 8-10 hours. Give the stew a good stir every 2-3 hours, if possible. Stir in the hand torn baby spinach during the last 30 minutes of cooking time. If stew becomes too thick add in a little extra vegetable broth to reach desired consistency. Remove cinnamon stick, taste and adjust seasonings as desired and serve with a sprinkle of fresh chopped parsley. Makes 6-8 servings. *I like to add in a little extra splash of apple cider vinegar right before serving, as I find it really helps to heighten the sharpness of all the aromatic spices.

Layered Mushroom and Potato Stew

Ingredients:

1 large yellow onion (diced)

4 large potatoes (any variety - peeled and rough chopped)

2 large carrots (diced)

16 ounces of white button mushrooms (sliced)

2 large bay leaves

1 cup tomato sauce

1-1/2 cups vegetable broth

5 tablespoons quick-cooking tapioca (dry measurement)

4 fresh garlic cloves (minced)

1-1/2 tablespoons Worcestershire sauce

1 teaspoon dried thyme

1 teaspoon sea salt

1 teaspoon ground black pepper

1/2 teaspoon dried oregano

2 cups green peas

* fresh chopped parsley for garnish

Evenly spread the diced onion into the bottom of your slow cooker. Next, evenly layer the chopped potatoes on top, followed by the diced carrots and sliced mushrooms. Place the 2 bay leaves on top of the layered vegetables.

In a mixing bowl, whisk together all of the remaining ingredients EXCEPT the green peas until well blended. Slowly pour the mixture on top of the layered vegetables in your slow cooker and do NOT stir at this point. Cook on "low" for 6-8 hours. During the last 1 hour of cooking time, give the stew a good stir while adding in the green peas. If stew becomes too thick, add in some more vegetable broth to reach desired consistency. Remove bay leaves and taste and adjust seasonings as desired before serving with a sprinkle of fresh chopped parsley. Makes 4-6 servings.

Tex-Mex Tempeh and Black Bean Stew

Ingredients:

2 packages of tempeh strips (you want about 1 pounds worth - cut into chunks)

1 can (15 ounce) black beans (rinsed and drained)

1 cup corn

1/2 cup diced red bell pepper

1/2 cup diced green chile peppers (if using canned green chiles, drain well first)

1/2 cup diced red onions

1 cup of your favorite salsa

12-14 ounces vegetable broth

2 fresh garlic cloves (minced)

1-1/2 teaspoons ground cumin

1/2 teaspoon chili powder

1/2 teaspoon dried thyme

1/2 teaspoon sea salt

1/2 teaspoon ground black pepper

* fresh chopped cilantro for garnish

Combine all of the ingredients in your slow cooker. Stir very thoroughly to blend and cook on "low" for 6-8 hours. If stew becomes too thick, add in some more vegetable broth to reach desired consistency. Taste and adjust seasoning as desired before serving with a sprinkle of fresh chopped cilantro. You can serve as-is, or over fresh steamed rice. Makes 4 servings.

Polynesian Stew

Ingredients:

3 tablespoons olive oil

1 yellow onion (diced)

3 fresh garlic cloves (minced)

1/2 of a large head of cauliflower (cut into small florets)

2 large golden russet potatoes (peeled and cubed)

1 can (15 ounce) chickpeas (rinsed and drained)

1 cup coconut milk

3/4 cup vegetable broth (or more, as needed)

1 teaspoon fresh grated ginger root

1 teaspoon ground cumin

1 teaspoon ground curry

1 teaspoon dried thyme

1/2 teaspoon ground turmeric

1/2 teaspoon ground coriander

1/2 teaspoon sea salt

1/2 teaspoon ground black pepper

1/4 teaspoon cayenne pepper

* fresh chopped parsley or cilantro for garnish

Combine all of the ingredients in your slow cooker. Stir well to blend and cook on "low" for 6 hours. Taste and adjust seasonings as desired before serving as-is or over fresh steamed rice with a sprinkle of fresh chopped parsley or cilantro. Makes 4 servings.

Curried Chickpea, Potato and Veggie Stew

Ingredients:

3 tablespoons olive oil

1 large yellow onion (diced)

1 cup sliced carrots

3 fresh garlic cloves (minced)

1 serrano pepper (seeded and diced)

1 tablespoon curry powder

1 teaspoon fresh grated ginger root

1 teaspoon brown sugar

2 cans (15 ounces each) chickpeas (rinsed and drained)

1-1/2 cups peeled, diced potato

1-1/2 cups diced tomatoes

1 cup diced green bell pepper

1 cup diced green beans

2-1/2 to 3 cups vegetable broth

1 teaspoon sea salt

1/2 teaspoon ground black pepper

1/4 teaspoon crushed red pepper flakes

3 cups chopped fresh baby spinach

1 cup coconut milk

* fresh chopped parsley for garnish

Heat the olive oil in a skillet over medium heat. Add in the diced onions and carrots and saute for 5 minutes. Add in the minced garlic, diced serrano pepper, curry powder, grated ginger root and brown sugar and stir continuously until fragrant, about 30-60 seconds. Transfer the sauteed mixture into your slow cooker along with all of the remaining ingredients EXCEPT the spinach and coconut milk. Stir well to blend and cook on "low" for 6-7 hours. Stir in the spinach and coconut milk during the last 30 minutes of cooking time. Taste and adjust seasonings as desired before serving as-is or over fresh steamed rice with a sprinkle of fresh chopped parsley. Makes 4-6 servings.

Chapter 5 –
Slow Cooker Recipes: Chilis

Spicy Chipotle Chocolate Chili

Ingredients:

¼ cup olive oil

1 large yellow onion (diced)

3 tablespoons ground chili powder

2 tablespoons ground cumin

2 teaspoons ground coriander

2 teaspoons ground oregano

2 teaspoons ground cinnamon

2 teaspoons sea salt

½ teaspoon ground black pepper

6-8 fresh garlic cloves (minced)

2-1/2 cups diced tomatoes

1 cup vegetable broth OR water

2 can chipotle chilies in adobe sauce (rough chopped)

1-2 jalapeno peppers (seeded and diced)

1 bottle (12 ounces) of dark beer (may substitute with 12 ounces of vegetable broth or water)

6 ounces tomato paste

1 can (15 ounces) pinto beans (WITH liquid)

1 can (15 ounces) kidney beans (WITH liquid)

1 can (15 ounces) black beans (WITH liquid)

2 tablespoons fresh squeezed lime juice

2-3 ounces of bittersweet baking chocolate (shaved)

Heat the olive oil on "high" in the slow cooker until thoroughly warmed. Add in the diced onion, cover and cook for about 10-15 minutes, or until onions are translucent. Add in all of the spices and minced garlic and cook for an additional 5 minutes, stirring frequently so that the spices and garlic do not burn. Add in the diced tomatoes, vegetable broth (or water) and chopped chipotle chilies with their sauce, stir to blend and keeping the slow cooker setting on "high" allow the mixture to come to a boil, again stirring frequently to prevent any of the ingredients from burning or sticking to the bottom.

Once the mixture comes to a low boil, immediately stir in the beer and tomato paste, and keep stirring until the tomato paste becomes thinned out. Once the tomato sauce has thinned, stir in all of the beans along with their liquid and the lime juice, lower the heat setting to "low" and cook for 45 minutes. Next, add in the shaved baking chocolate and stir until thoroughly melted. Recover, and continue cooking on "low" heat setting for 4 hours. If you will be away at work and school and need to leave the slow cooker on for more than 4 hours, follow all of the directions the same, but add in an extra 1/2 cup of liquid (water, vegetable broth or beer) to prevent the chili from getting too thick and pasty. Serve with your favorite chili toppings: tortilla chips; sour cream; shredded cheese; minced onions; fresh chopped cilantro, etc.. Makes 6-8 servings.

Cowboy Chipotle Chili

Ingredients:

2 cans (15 ounce) black beans (rinsed and drained)

2 cans (15 ounce) white kidney beans (rinsed and drained)

4 cups diced tomatoes

1 large yellow onion (diced)

1-2 jalapeno peppers (seeded and diced)

2 cups vegetable broth or water (or more, as needed)

6-8 fresh garlic cloves (minced)

2 teaspoon chipotle chiles (minced)

4 tablespoons chili powder

2 tablespoons paprika

2 tablespoons dried cilantro

1 teaspoon ground black pepper

Combine all of the ingredients in your slow cooker, stir to blend and cook on "low" for 6 hours. Serve with your favorite chili toppings and/or freshly baked cornbread. Makes 8 servings.

Sweet and Nutty Veggie and Bean Chili

Ingredients:

4 tablespoons olive oil

2 yellow onions (diced)

2 large carrots (grated or finely diced)

2 green bell peppers (seeded and diced)

8 ounces thinly sliced mushrooms (any variety)

3 fresh garlic cloves (minced)

2 cans (15 ounce each) red kidney beans (rinsed and drained)

4 cups diced tomatoes

1 cup vegetable broth or water (or more, as needed)

1 cup chopped cashews

1/4 cup sesame seeds (optional)

1/4 cup chopped raisins

1 teaspoon dried oregano

1 teaspoon dried basil

1 teaspoon cumin

1-2 teaspoons chili powder

1 large bay leaf

1/2 teaspoon sea salt

1/2 teaspoon ground black pepper

splash of balsamic vinegar

Heat the olive oil in a skillet over medium heat. Add in the onions, carrots, bell peppers and mushrooms and saute until onions are translucent, about 4 minutes. Add in the minced garlic and stir continuously while sauteeing until fragrant, about 30-60 seconds. Remove from heat.

Add the sauteed vegetable mixture into your slow cooker along with all of the remaining ingredients, stir to blend and cook on "low" for 6 hours. Start with 1 cup of the vegetable broth or water, and then add more as needed to desired chili thickness and consistency. Remove bay leaf and serve with your favorite chili toppings and/or freshly baked cornbread. Makes 4 servings.

Thick and Chunky Zesty Chili

Ingredients:

1/2 cup olive oil

4 yellow onions (diced)

2 large green bell peppers (seeded and diced)

2 large red bell peppers (seeded and diced)

6 fresh garlic cloves (minced)

1 package (14 ounce) extra-firm tofu (pressed, drained and diced)

2 cans (15 ounces each) black beans (rinsed and drained)

2 cans (15 ounces each) red kidney beans (rinsed and drained)

2-1/2 cups diced tomatoes

1 cup vegetable broth or water

5-6 tablespoons chili powder

2 tablespoons dried oregano

2 tablespoons vinegar (balsamic or apple cider vinegar)

1 tablespoon of your favorite hot sauce (or, to heat and taste preference)

2 teaspoons ground cumin

2 teaspoons sea salt

1/2 teaspoon ground black pepper

Heat the olive oil in a skillet over medium heat. Add in the diced onions and saute until they start to become translucent, about 4 minutes. Stir in both the green and red bell peppers, minced garlic and diced tofu and stir frequently while cooking for an additional 4-5 minutes.

Transfer the sauteed vegetable mixture along with all of the remaining ingredients into your slow cooker. Stir well to blend and then cook on "low" for 6-8 hours. Makes 6-8 servings.

Taco Style Chili

Ingredients:

3-4 tablespoons olive oil

1 yellow onion (diced)

16 ounces thinly sliced mushrooms (any variety)

4 fresh garlic cloves (minced)

1/2 of a large green bell pepper (diced)

2 cans (15 ounces each) black beans (rinsed and drained)

1 can (15 ounces) red kidney beans (rinsed and drained)

2 cans (15 ounces each) tomato sauce (I use Muir Glen organic tomato sauce)

1 can (6 ounces) tomato paste

1-1/2 cups of corn

1/2 teaspoon chili powder

1/2 teaspoon cumin powder

1/2 teaspoon ground oregano

pinch of crushed red pepper flakes

pinch of ground black pepper

Heat the olive oil in a skillet over medium heat. Add in the diced onion and saute until onions start to become translucent, about 4 minutes. Stir in the sliced mushrooms, minced garlic and diced green bell pepper and stir frequently while cooking for an additional 4-5 minutes. Remove from heat.

Transfer the sauteed vegetable mixture along with all of the remaining ingredients into your slow cooker. Stir well to blend and cook on "low" for 6 hours. Taste and adjust seasoning towards the end of the cooking time, as desired. Serve with your favorite chili toppings and/or some fresh baked cornbread or warm French bread. Makes 6 servings.

Three Bean Spicy Cajun Chili

Ingredients:

2-1/2 cups vegetable broth (or more as needed)

2 cans (15 ounces each) black beans (rinsed and drained)

2 cans (15 ounces each) red kidney beans (rinsed and drained)

2 cans (15 ounces each) cannellini beans (rinsed and drained)

2 cups diced tomatoes

4 fresh garlic cloves (minced)

1 large jalapeno pepper (seeded and diced)

2 tablespoons chili powder

4 teaspoons Cajun seasoning blend

1-2 tablespoons fresh lime juice

Combine all of the ingredients EXCEPT the lime juice into your slow cooker. Stir well to blend and cook on "low" for 6-8 hours. If chili becomes too thick for your liking, add in more vegetable broth. Stir in the lime juice just before serving. Serve with your favorite chili toppings. Makes 6-8 servings.

Sweet and Spicy Pumpkin Chili

Ingredients:

1 can (15 ounce) black beans (rinsed and drained)

1 bag (12 ounces) of meatless crumbles (I typically use Morningstar or Boca brands)

1 yellow onion (diced)

3 cups diced tomatoes

1 cup pumpkin puree

1 bottle (12 ounces) of chili sauce (I use Organicville)

1-2 tablespoons chili powder

2 teaspoons pumpkin pie spice

1-1/2 teaspoons sea salt

1 teaspoon ground black pepper

* water as needed, if chili becomes too thick

Combine all of the ingredients in your slow cooker. Stir well to blend and cook on "low" for 4 hours. If chili becomes too thick for your liking during cooking time, add in a little water to reach desired consistency. Serve with your favorite chili toppings. Makes 4 servings.

Southern Style Chili

Ingredients:

1 cup vegetable broth (or more, if needed)

1/2 tomato paste

2 teaspoons chili powder

1 teaspoon ground cumin

1/2 teaspoon dried oregano

1/2 teaspoon ground black pepper

1/4 teaspoon of ground mustard powder

2 cans (15 ounces each) red kidney beans (rinsed and drained)

2 cans (15 ounce) white kidney beans (rinsed and drained)

1 large yellow onion (diced)

1 whole jalapeno pepper (seeded and diced)

2 cups diced tomatoes

1 cup corn

*Optional: If you desire more "heat", add in some crushed red pepper flakes.

Combine the vegetable broth, tomato paste, chili powder, cumin, oregano, black pepper and mustard powder into your slow cooker. Whisk to blend all of the spices and the tomato paste thins a bit. Add in all of the remaining ingredients, stir well to blend and cook on "low" for 6-8 hours. If chili becomes too thick during cooking time, add in more vegetable broth to reach desired consistency. Serve with your favorite chili toppings. Makes 4 servings.

Tex-Mex Mock Beef Chili

Ingredients:

4 tablespoons olive oil

1 large yellow onion (diced)

6 fresh garlic cloves (minced)

2 packages (12 ounces each) veggie crumbles (I typically use MorningStar or LightLife Smart Ground)

2 cans (15 ounces each) pinto beans (rinsed and drained)

3 cups diced tomatoes

1/2 cup corn

1-1/2 cups chunky salsa

1/2 cup vegetable broth

1 tablespoon ground cumin

4 teaspoons chili powder

sea salt and black pepper (to taste)

1 cup finely shredded Mexican cheese blend

1/4 cup chopped black olives

Heat the olive oil in a skillet over medium heat. Add in the diced onions and saute until onions become translucent, about 4 minutes. Add in the minced garlic and stir continuously until fragrant, about

30-60 seconds. Transfer the sauteed onion-garlic mixture into your slow cooker along with all of the remaining ingredients EXCEPT the shredded cheese and black olives. Stir well to blend and cook on "low" for 6-7 hours. If chili becomes too thick during cooking time, add in a little extra vegetable broth to reach desired consistency. Taste and adjust seasonings as desired and serve each bowl topped with some of the shredded cheesed and chopped black olives, along with any other of your favorite chili toppings. Makes 8 servings.

Jamaican Black-Eyed Pea Chili

Ingredients:

1 cup diced onions

3-4 green chile peppers (seeded and diced)

3-4 fresh garlic cloves (minced)

2 cans (15 ounces each) black-eye-peas (rinsed and drained)

1-1/2 cups diced tomatoes

1 cup finely diced green bell pepper

1 cup finely diced carrots

1 cup orange juice

3/4 cup vegetable broth

4 teaspoons chili powder

1-1/2 teaspoons ground cumin

2 tablespoons dried cilantro

2 tablespoons water

1 tablespoon cornstarch

* fresh chopped cilantro for garnish

Combine all of the ingredients in your slow cooker EXCEPT the water and cornstarch. Stir well to blend and cook on "low" for 6-8 hours. Whisk together the water and cornstarch to make a slurry. Stir the cornstarch slurry into the chili during the last 30 minutes of cooking time. Taste and adjust seasonings as desired, and add sea salt and black pepper to taste (if desired). Serve with a sprinkle of fresh chopped cilantro. Makes 4-6 servings.

Zesty Pumpkin, Pinto and Veggie Chili

Ingredients:

3 tablespoons olive oil

1 large yellow onion (diced)

4-5 fresh garlic cloves (minced)

1 small jalapeno pepper (seeded and diced)

1 cup diced mushrooms (any variety)

1-1/2 cups peeled, cubed pumpkin (you may substitute with squash if pumpkin is not in season)

1 cup corn

1-1/2 cups diced tomatoes

3 cans (15 ounces each) pinto beans (rinsed and drained)

1 cup vegetable broth (or more, as needed)

1 tablespoon ground cumin

1 teaspoon raw sugar

3/4 teaspoon sea salt

1/2 teaspoon ground black pepper

* raw or roasted pumpkin seeds for garnish

Heat the olive oil in a skillet over medium heat. Add in the diced onions and saute until onions become translucent, about 4 minutes. Add in the minced garlic, jalapeno pepper and diced mushrooms and stir continuously while cooking for an additional 1-2 minutes.

Transfer the sauteed mixture into your slow cooker along with all of the remaining ingredients. Stir well to blend and cook on "low" for 6-8 hours. If chili becomes too thick, stir in a little extra vegetable broth to reach desired consistency. Taste and adjust seasonings as desired before serving with a sprinkle of pumpkin seeds and your favorite chili toppings. Makes 6-8 servings.

Spicy Red Bean and Veggie Chili

Ingredients:

3 tablespoons olive oil

1 large yellow onion (diced)

5 fresh garlic cloves (minced)

1 jalapeno pepper (seeded and diced)

1 large green bell pepper (seeded and diced)

1 large red bell pepper (seeded and diced)

1 cup diced celery

1 large zucchini (peeled and cubed)

3 cups diced tomatoes

3 cans (15 ounces each) red kidney beans (rinsed and drained)

1 can (6 ounce) tomato paste

1/2 cup tomato sauce

1 cup vegetable broth (or more, as needed)

1-1/2 tablespoons chili powder

1 tablespoon dried oregano

4 teaspoons ground cumin

1 teaspoon paprika (regular or smoked)

1 teaspoon sea salt

1 teaspoon ground black pepper

1/2 teaspoon crushed red pepper flakes

* fresh chopped cilantro for garnish

Heat the olive oil in a skillet over medium heat. Add in the minced garlic and diced jalapeno pepper and stir continuously until fragrant, about 30-60 seconds. Transfer the sauteed mixture into your slow cooker along with all of the remaining ingredients. Stir very thoroughly to blend and cook on "low" for 6-8 hours. If chili becomes too thick, add in some more vegetable broth to reach desired consistency. Taste and adjust seasonings as desired before serving with a sprinkle of fresh chopped cilantro and your favorite chili toppings. This is a spicy chili, so I recommend "cooling" toppings such as sour cream, Greek style yogurt, shredded cheese, fresh lime wedges, etc., to balance out the heat while still enjoying the spicy delicious flavors. Makes 8 servings.

Sweet and Chunky Hominy, Bean and Mock Beef Chili

Ingredients:

3 tablespoons olive oil

1 large yellow onion (diced)

4-5 fresh garlic cloves (minced)

1 small jalapeno pepper (seeded and diced)

3 cups corn

2-1/2 cups diced tomatoes

2 cans (15 ounces each) red kidney beans (rinsed and drained)

2 cans (15 ounces each) white kidney beans (rinsed and drained)

1 can (15 ounce) hominy (rinsed and drained)

1 package (12-14 ounce) veggie crumbles (I use MorningStar brand)

1 can (15 ounce) tomato sauce

1 can (6 ounce) tomato paste

2 tablespoons pure maple syrup

6 tablespoons nutritional yeast (adds cheese flavor)

1 tablespoon ground cumin

1 tablespoon dried oregano

2-3 teaspoons chili powder

2 teaspoons sea salt

1 teaspoon ground black pepper

1/2 cup vegetable broth (or more, to desired consistency)

Heat the olive oil in a skillet over medium heat. Add in the diced onions and saute until onions become translucent, about 4 minutes. Add in the minced garlic and jalapeno peppers and stir continuously until fragrant, about 30-60 seconds. Transfer the sauteed mixture into your slow cooker along with all of the remaining ingredients. Stir very thoroughly to blend and cook on "low" for 6-8 hours, stirring every 2-3 hours if possible. If chili becomes too thick add in some more vegetable broth to reach desired consistency. Taste and adjust seasonings as desired before serving with your favorite chili toppings. Makes 8 servings.

Smoked Bac'Un and Bean Chili

Ingredients:

3 tablespoons olive oil

1 large yellow onion (diced)

4 fresh garlic cloves (minced)

1 cup diced green bell peppers

1 cup diced carrots

4-1/2 cups diced tomatoes

3 cans (15 ounces each) pinto beans (rinsed and drained)

2 cups vegetable broth (or more, as needed)

1 can (6 ounce) tomato paste

1/4 cup vegan Bac'Un bits

1-1/2 tablespoons liquid smoke

1 tablespoon Worcestershire sauce

1 tablespoon chili powder

2 teaspoons dried oregano

1/2-1 teaspoon crushed red pepper flakes

sea salt and black pepper (to taste)

Heat the olive oil in a skillet over medium heat. Add in the diced onions and saute until onions become translucent, about 4 minutes. Add in the minced garlic and stir continuously until fragrant, about 30-60 seconds. Transfer the sauteed onion-garlic mixture into your slow cooker along with all of the remaining ingredients. Stir very thoroughly to blend and cook on "low" for 6-8 hours, stirring every 2-3 hours if possible. Taste and adjust seasonings as desired before serving with your favorite chili toppings. Makes 6-8 servings.

Easy Go-To Mock Meat Chili

Ingredients:

3 tablespoons olive oil

2 large yellow onions (diced)

2 large green bell peppers (seeded and diced)

6 fresh garlic cloves (minced)

2 bags (12 ounces each) veggie crumbles

2 cans (15 ounces each) pinto beans (rinsed and drained)

2 cans (15 ounces each) red kidney beans (rinsed and drained)

2 cups diced tomatoes

1-1/2 cups vegetable broth

1-1/2 teaspoons chili powder

1 teaspoon ground cumin

1 teaspoon ground oregano

1 teaspoon sea salt

1/2 teaspoon ground black pepper

drizzle of balsamic vinegar

Heat the olive oil in a skillet over medium heat. Add in the diced onions and green peppers and saute until onions become translucent, about 4 minutes. Add in the minced garlic and stir continuously until fragrant, about 30-60 seconds. Transfer sauteed vegetable mixture into your slow cooker along with all of the remaining ingredients. Stir well to blend and cook on "low" for 6-8 hours. If chili becomes too thick, add in a little extra vegetable broth to reach desired consistency. Taste and adjust seasonings as desired before serving with your favorite chili toppings. Makes 6-8 servings.

Chunky Chick'n and Green Chile Chili

Ingredients:

1 pound of northern beans (dry measurement)

3 tablespoons olive oil

1 large yellow onion (diced)

4-5 fresh garlic cloves (minced)

4 green chile peppers (seeded and diced)

5 packages (6 ounces each) of LightLife Chick'n strips (chopped)

6 cups vegetable broth

2 teaspoons ground cumin

1 teaspoon chili powder

1 teaspoon ground oregano

1 teaspoon sea salt

1/4 teaspoon crushed red pepper flakes

2 tablespoons cornmeal

1 cup vegetable broth

* fresh chopped parsley or cilantro for garnish

Soak the northern beans overnight. The next morning drain, rinse and drain again.

Heat the olive oil in a skillet over medium heat. Add in the diced onion and saute until onions become translucent, about 4 minutes.

Add in the minced garlic and diced green chiles and stir continuously until fragrant, about 30-60 seconds. Transfer the sauteed mixture into your slow cooker, along with the soaked, rinsed beans and all of the remaining ingredients EXCEPT the cornstarch and 1 cup of vegetable broth. Stir very thoroughly to blend all ingredients and cook on "low" for 6-8 hours. In a mixing bowl, whisk together the cornstarch and 1 cup of vegetable broth. Stir this mixture into the chili during the last 45-60 minutes of cooking time. Taste and adjust seasonings as desired before serving with a sprinkle of fresh chopped parsley or cilantro. Makes 8 servings.

Mock Beef and Chorizo Chili

Ingredients:

3 tablespoons olive oil

1 large yellow onion (diced)

3-4 fresh garlic cloves (minced)

1 jalapeno pepper (seeded and diced)

1 package (12 ounces) veggie crumbles

1 package (12 ounces) veggie chorizo (diced)

3 cans (15 ounces each) pinto beans (rinsed and drained)

3 cups vegetable broth

2 cups diced tomatoes

1 can (6 ounce) tomato paste

1 tablespoon chili powder

2 teaspoons ground cumin

2 teaspoons dried oregano

sea salt and black pepper (to taste)

* fresh chopped cilantro for garnish

Heat the olive oil in a skillet over medium heat. Add in the diced onions and saute until onions become translucent, about 4 minutes. Add in the minced garlic and diced jalapeno peppers, and stir continuously until fragrant, about 30-60 seconds. Transfer the sauteed mixture into your slow cooker along with all of the remaining ingredients. Stir very thoroughly to blend and cook on "low" for 4-6 hours. If chili becomes too thick, add in a little extra vegetable broth to reach desired consistency. Taste and adjust seasonings as desired before serving with a sprinkle of fresh chopped cilantro and your favorite chili toppings. Makes 6-8 servings.

Lentil and Red Bean Chili

Ingredients:

1 pound brown lentils (dry measurement)

3 tablespoons olive oil

1 large yellow onion (diced)

4 fresh garlic cloves (minced)

1 jalapeno pepper (seeded and diced)

1 large red bell pepper (seeded and diced)

1 large green bell pepper (seeded and diced)

1 large carrot (diced)

2 cups diced tomatoes

3 cups vegetable broth

2 cups tomato sauce

1 can (6 ounces) tomato paste

2 cans (15 ounces each) red kidney beans (rinsed and drained)

2 tablespoons chili powder

1 tablespoon dried oregano

2 teaspoons ground cumin

1 teaspoon ground black pepper

1 teaspoon sea salt

* fresh chopped parsley for garnish

Soak the lentils for 15-30 minutes. Drain, rinse and drain again.

Heat the olive oil in a skillet over medium heat. Add in the diced onions and saute until translucent, about 4 minutes. Add in the minced garlic and diced jalapeno pepper, and stir continuously until fragrant, about 30-60 seconds. Transfer the sauteed mixture into your slow cooker along with the soaked, drained lentils and all of the remaining ingredients. Stir well to blend and cook on "low" for 6-8 hours, or until lentils are nice and tender. Taste and adjust seasonings as desired before serving with a sprinkle of fresh chopped parsley and your favorite chili toppings. Makes 8 servings.

Mock Turkey and Bean Chili

Ingredients:

3 tablespoons olive oil

1 large yellow onion (diced)

3-4 fresh garlic cloves (minced)

3 green chile peppers (seeded and diced)

2 large red bell peppers (seeded and diced)

2 packages (12 ounces each) vegetarian ground turkey (I use Yves brand)

2 cups diced tomatoes

2 cans (15 ounces each) cannellini beans (rinsed and drained)

2 cans (15 ounces each) black beans (rinsed and drained)

3 cups tomato sauce

1 cups vegetable broth

1 can (6 ounce) tomato paste

1 cup corn

2 tablespoons chili powder

1 tablespoon ground cumin

1 tablespoon dried oregano

1 teaspoon sea salt

1/2 teaspoon ground black pepper

* fresh chopped parsley or cilantro for garnish

Heat the olive oil in a skillet over medium heat. Add in the diced onion and saute until onion becomes translucent, about 4 minutes. Add in the minced garlic and diced jalapeno peppers, and stir continuously until fragrant, about 30-60 seconds. Transfer the sauteed mixture into your slow cooker along with all of the remaining ingredients. Stir very thoroughly to blend and cook on "low" for about 6 hours. If chili becomes too thick, add in a little extra vegetable broth or tomato sauce to reach desired consistency. Taste and adjust seasonings as desired before serving with a sprinkle of fresh chopped parsley or cilantro and your favorite chili toppings. Makes 8 servings.

Mock Picante Beef and Bean Chili

Ingredients:

3 tablespoons olive oil

1 large yellow onion (diced)

4 fresh garlic cloves (minced)

1 jalapeno pepper (seeded and diced)

1 whole bag + 1/2 of a bag (12 ounces each) of veggie crumbles

1 can (15 ounce) pinto beans (rinsed and drained)

1 can (15 ounce) black beans (rinsed and drained)

1 can (15 ounce) refried beans (most are vegetarian, but check the label)

2-1/4 cups picante sauce (medium heat)

2-1/4 cups vegetable broth

1 tablespoon chili powder

2 teaspoons ground cumin

2 teaspoon dried oregano

1 teaspoon sea salt

1/2 teaspoon ground black pepper

2 tablespoons fresh squeezed lime juice

* fresh chopped cilantro and lime wedges for garnish

Heat the olive oil in a skillet over medium heat. Add in the diced onions and saute until onions become translucent, about 4 minutes. Add in the minced garlic and diced jalapeno peppers, and stir continuously until fragrant, about 30-60 seconds. Transfer the sauteed mixture into your slow cooker along with all of the remaining ingredients EXCEPT the lime juice. Stir very thoroughly to blend and cook on "low" for about 6 hours. If chili becomes too thick, add in a little extra vegetable broth to reach desired consistency. Taste and adjust seasonings as desired and stir in the lime juice just before serving with a sprinkle of fresh chopped cilantro and lime wedge for garnish. Makes 4-6 servings.

Chick'n Enchilada Chili

Ingredients:

3 tablespoons olive oil

1 large yellow onion (diced)

3-4 fresh garlic cloves (minced)

1 jalapeno pepper (seeded and diced)

3 packages (12 ounces each) LightLife Chick'n strips (diced)

1-1/2 cups tomato sauce

1 vegetable broth

1 can (6 ounce) tomato paste

2 cans (15 ounces each) black beans (rinsed and drained)

2 cups diced tomatoes

1-1/2 cups corn

2 tablespoons chili powder

1 tablespoon ground cumin

1 tablespoon dried oregano

1 tablespoon raw sugar

1 teaspoon sea salt

1 teaspoon ground black pepper

* toppings to assemble finished chili: shredded Mexican blend cheese; sliced black olives; chopped cilantro and sour cream

Combine all of the ingredients in your slow cooker. Stir very thoroughly to blend all ingredients and cook on "low" for 6-8 hours. If chili becomes too thick, add in a little extra vegetable broth or tomato sauce to reach desired consistency. Taste and adjust seasonings as desired and serve each bowl of chili topped with some of the shredded cheese, black olives, chopped cilantro and sour cream. Makes 6 servings.

White Bean and Veggie Chili

Ingredients:

3 tablespoons olive oil

1 large yellow onion (diced)

2 large celery stalks (diced)

2 large carrots (thinly sliced)

4 fresh garlic cloves (minced)

1 pound of thinly sliced mushrooms (any variety)

2 large zucchini (peeled and diced)

2-1/2 cups diced tomatoes

1-1/2 cups corn

4 cans (15 ounces each) cannellini beans (rinsed and drained)

3 cups tomato sauce

2 cups vegetable broth

1 can (6 ounce) tomato paste

1-1/2 tablespoons chili powder

1 tablespoon ground cumin

1 tablespoon dried oregano

1 teaspoon sea salt

1 teaspoon ground black pepper

* fresh chopped parsley or cilantro for garnish

Heat the olive oil in a large skillet over medium heat. Add in the diced onions, celery and carrots and saute for 5 minutes. Add in the minced garlic and stir continuously until fragrant, about 30-60 seconds. Transfer sauteed mixture into your slow cooker along with all of the remaining ingredients. Stir very thoroughly to blend and cook on "low" for 6-8 hours. If chili becomes too thick, add in a little extra tomato sauce or vegetable broth to reach desired consistency. Taste and adjust seasonings as desired before serving with a sprinkle of fresh chopped parsley or cilantro. Makes 6-8 servings.

Chick'n - Jalapeno Popper Chili

Ingredients:

1 pound northern beans (dry measurement)

3 tablespoons olive oil

1 large yellow onion (diced)

4 fresh garlic cloves (minced)

2 jalapeno peppers (seeded and diced)

2 large red bell peppers (seeded and diced)

2 packages (12 ounces each) vegetarian chick'n strips (diced - I use LightLife brand)

2 cups diced tomatoes

5 cups vegetable broth

1 tablespoon chili powder

2 teaspoons ground cumin

2 teaspoons dried oregano

1/2 teaspoon sea salt

1/2 teaspoon ground black pepper

1 package (8 ounces) cream cheese (regular or vegan - cut into diced sized pieces)

2 cups corn

1/2 cup vegan Bac'n bits

Soak the beans overnight in water. The next morning, drain, rinse and drain again.

Heat the olive oil in a skillet over medium heat. Add in the diced onions and saute until onions are translucent, about 4 minutes. Add in the minced garlic and diced jalapeno peppers, and stir continuously until fragrant, about 30-60 seconds. Transfer the sauteed mixture into your slow cooker along with the soaked, rinsed beans and all of the remaining ingredients EXCEPT the cream cheese, corn and Bac'n bits. Stir very thoroughly to blend all ingredients and cook on "low" for 6-8 hours. If chili becomes too thick, add in a little extra vegetable broth to reach desired consistency. Stir in the cream cheese, corn and Bac'n bits during the last 1 hours of cooking time. Taste and adjust seasonings as desired before serving. Makes 6-8 servings. * If chili is too thin for your liking, whisk together a little cornstarch and vegetable broth to make a slurry and stir into chili at a ratio of 1 tablespoon cornstarch to ½ cup of vegetable broth.

Fireside Chili

Ingredients:

3 tablespoons olive oil

1 large yellow onion (diced)

1 large green bell pepper (seeded and diced)

1 large red bell pepper (seeded and diced)

4-6 fresh garlic cloves (minced)

3 bags (12 ounces each) veggie crumbles

3 cups vegetable broth

3 cups tomato sauce

2 cans (6 ounces each) tomato paste

2 cans (15 ounces each) pinto beans (rinsed and drained)

2 tablespoons chili powder

1-1/2 tablespoon ground cumin

1-1/2 tablespoon dried oregano

1 tablespoon Braggs liquid aminos (you may also use Tamari or regular soy sauce)

1 teaspoon sea salt

1/4 teaspoon crushed red pepper flakes

Heat the olive oil in a skillet over medium heat. Add in the diced onions and diced green and red bell pepper, and saute while stirring frequently for 5 minutes. Add in the minced garlic and stir continuously until fragrant, about 30-60 seconds. Transfer the sauteed mixture into your slow cooker along with all of the remaining ingredients. Stir very thoroughly to blend all ingredients and cook on "low" for about 6 hours. If chili becomes too thick, add in some extra vegetable broth or tomato sauce to reach desired consistency. Taste and adjust seasonings as desired before serving. Makes 6-8 servings.

Hot and Hearty Mock Meat Lovers Chili

Ingredients:

3-4 tablespoons olive oil

2 yellow onions (diced)

6 fresh garlic cloves (minced)

1 jalapeno pepper (seeded and diced)

2 packages (5 ounces each) vegetarian bacon (diced)

3 packages (12 ounces each) veggie crumbles

4 cans (15 ounces each) red kidney beans (rinsed and drained)

3 cups diced tomatoes

2 cans (6 ounces each) tomato paste

2 cups vegetable broth

3 tablespoons chili powder

1 tablespoon ground cumin

1 tablespoon dried oregano

1 tablespoon smoked paprika

1 teaspoon crushed red pepper flakes

1 teaspoon sea salt

Heat the olive oil in a skillet over medium heat. Add in the diced onions and saute until onions become translucent, about 4 minutes. Add in the minced garlic and diced jalapeno peppers and stir continuously until fragrant, about 30-60 seconds. Transfer sauteed mixture into your slow cooker along with all of the remaining ingredients. Stir very thoroughly to blend and cook on "low" for 6-8 hours, stirring regularly every couple of hours. If chili becomes too thick add in a little extra vegetable broth to reach desired consistency. Taste and adjust seasonings as desired before serving with your favorite chili toppings. Makes 8-10 servings.

Chapter 6 –
Slow Cooker Recipes:
Sides

Caribbean Style Black Beans

Ingredients:

4 cans (15 ounces each) black beans (rinsed and drained)

2 cups diced pineapple (if using canned pineapple thoroughly rinse and drain first)

8 vegetarian sausage links (diced)

1 large yellow onion (diced)

1 cup of your favorite barbeque sauce

2/3 cup brown sugar

2 heaping tablespoons freshly grated ginger root

2 tablespoons fresh squeezed lime juice

pinch of fresh lime zest

3 teaspoons dry mustard powder

sea salt and black pepper to taste

1/3-1/2 cup vegetable broth or water (more, as needed)

Combine all of the ingredients in a large slow cooker and cook on "low" for 4-6 hours. If mixture becomes too dry, add in more vegetable broth or water. Makes 8 servings. Serves as a delicious side dish, or topped over fresh steamed rice for a hearty main meal.

Indian Lentils and Rice

Ingredients:

2 tablespoons olive oil

1 yellow onion (diced)

5-6 cups vegetable broth

1 cup brown lentils (dry measurement)

½ cup long-grain rice (dry measurement)

1 tablespoon ground cumin

½ teaspoon ground cinnamon

¾ teaspoon sea salt

Heat the olive oil in a skillet over medium heat. Once heated, add in the diced onion and sauté until onions are translucent, about 4-5 minutes. Transfer the sautéed onions into your slow cooker along with all of the remaining ingredients, stir to blend and cook on "low" for 8 hours. *Start with 5 cups of vegetable broth, and if mixture becomes too thick during cooking time add in more vegetable broth to reach desired consistency. I do not recommend starting out with more vegetable broth, because it's pretty difficult to correct mushy rice. Makes 4-6 servings.

Cracked Wheat Pilaf

Ingredients:

5 cups vegetable broth

2 cups cracked wheat (dry measurement)

1 yellow onion (diced)

2-1/2 tablespoons dried parsley

2 teaspoons sea salt

Combine all of the ingredients in your slow cooker, stir to blend and cook on "low" for 10-12 hours. Stir well before serving. Makes 6 servings.

Moroccan Cauliflower and Potatoes

Ingredients:

4 cups peeled and diced golden russet potatoes

1 small head of cauliflower (cored and cut into small florets)

2 large tomatoes (diced)

1-1/2 teaspoons ground cumin

¾ teaspoon garam marsala (Indian spice blend)

¾ teaspoon ground turmeric

¾ teaspoon sea salt

½ teaspoon chili powder

1-1/4 cup water

Combine all of the ingredients in your slow cooker, stir to blend and cook on "low" for 5-6 hours. Makes 6-8 servings.

Honey Ginger Lentils

Ingredients:

1-1/2 lentils (dry measurement, any variety)

3 cups vegetable broth

1/2 of a large red onion (diced)

1 can (15 ounce) chickpeas (rinsed and drained)

1/2 cup shredded carrots

2 tablespoons Braggs liquid aminos (you may also use Tamari or regular soy sauce)

1/3 cup + 2 tablespoons raw honey (divided - do not use commercially processed honey)

2 bay leaves

1 teaspoon ground mustard powder

1 teaspoon sea salt

1/4 teaspoon ground ginger

*freshly grated ginger for garnish (optional)

Thoroughly rinse and drain the lentils, and then add them along with all of the remaining ingredients EXCEPT the 2 extra tablespoons of raw honey into your slow cooker. Stir to blend and then cook on "low" for 6-8 hours. During the final 15-30 minutes of cooking time, remove the bay leaves and stir in the extra 2 tablespoons of raw honey. Serve as-is as a side dish, or over a bed of fresh steamed rice as a main meal. Sprinkle with some freshly grated ginger, optional. Makes 4-6 servings.

Easy Creamed Corn

Ingredients:

4 cups of corn

1 package (8 ounce) cream cheese (softened to room temperature and cut into cubes)

1 stick of butter (unsalted)

1/2 cup milk (regular or non-dairy)

1 tablespoon raw sugar

1 teaspoon paprika

1-2 fresh garlic cloves (minced)

sea salt and black pepper (to taste)

* minced green onion for garnish (optional)

Lightly grease bottom and sides of your slow cooker with oil or butter.

Combine all of the ingredients into your prepared slow cooker. Stir well to blend and cook on "low" for 4-6 hours, stirring every couple hours. Taste and adjust seasonings as desired before serving with an optional garnish of fresh minced green onion. Makes about 8 servings.

Spicy Coconut Baked Beans

Ingredients:

2 tablespoons olive oil

1 large yellow onion (diced)

3 fresh garlic cloves (minced)

1 tablespoon fresh grated ginger root

1 tablespoon of your favorite curry powder

1/2 teaspoon ground cumin

1/2 teaspoon sea salt

pinch of crushed red pepper flakes

1 can (14 ounce) coconut milk

1 can (6 ounce) tomato paste

2-3 tablespoons brown sugar

3 cans (15 ounces each) pinto beans (rinsed and drained)

Heat the olive oil in a saucepan over medium heat. Add in the diced onion and saute until the onions become translucent, about 4 minutes. Add in the minced garlic and grated ginger root and stir continuously while sauteeing for an additional 1 minute. Whisk in all of the remaining ingredients EXCEPT the beans, and stir while cooking until the tomato paste thins and blends with the other ingredients. Once the tomato paste has thinned, add the mixture along with the pinto beans into your slow cooker. Stir well to blend and cook on "low" for 8-10 hours. Makes 8 servings.

Stuffed Roasted Squash

Ingredients:

1 large acorn squash (halved and seeds and strings scooped out to make a hollow center in each half)

2 red variety apples (peeled and finely diced)

2 tablespoons brown sugar

2 tablespoons butter (melted)

1 tablespoon finely chopped nuts (walnuts or pecans)

1/2 teaspoon ground cinnamon

1/2 teaspoon sea salt

dash of ground nutmeg

In a mixing bowl, stir together all of the filling ingredients until well combined. Evenly spoon the mixture into the two prepared acorn squash halves and place the stuffed squash into the bottom of your slow cooker. Cook on "low" for about 6 hours, or until squash is fork tender. Makes 2-4 servings.

Sweet and Spicy Vegetables

Ingredients:

2 tablespoons olive oil

1 yellow onion (diced)

2 fresh garlic cloves (minced)

2-1/2 cups vegetable broth

1 large potato (peeled and cubed)

1 large apple (peeled, cored and diced)

3/4 cup cooked chickpeas (about 1/2 of a 15 ounce can - rinsed and drained)

1/2 cup diced carrots

1/3 of a head of green cabbage (cored and shredded)

3-4 celery stalks (diced)

a pinch of EACH: ground cinnamon; ground ginger; curry powder; cayenne pepper; sea salt; black pepper

1/2 of a can (14 ounce size) coconut milk

Heat the olive oil in a skillet over medium heat. Add in the diced onion and saute until onions start to become translucent, about 4 minutes. Add in the minced garlic and stir continuously until it becomes fragrant, about 30-60 seconds. Remove from heat and transfer onion-garlic mixture into your slow cooker along with all of the remaining ingredients EXCEPT the coconut milk. Stir well to blend and cook on "low" for 6-7 hours. Stir in the 1/2 can of coconut milk during the last 30 minutes of cooking time, along with any seasoning adjustments as desired. Makes 4-6 servings. I typically make this as a side dish, but it can also be served over a bed of fresh steamed rice as a main dish.

Wild Rice and Veggie Medley

Ingredients:

2-1/2 cups vegetable broth

1 cup wild rice (dry measurement - do NOT use an instant variety)

3 fresh garlic cloves (minced)

1 yellow onion (diced)

1 large carrot (diced – or thinly sliced)

1 large, or 2 small celery stalks (diced – or thinly sliced)

1/4 cup diced mushrooms (any variety will work, but I highly recommend shiitake or crimini variety)

3/4 teaspoon dried parsley

1/2 teaspoon sea salt

pinch of ground black pepper

Combine all of the ingredients in your slow cooker. Stir well to blend and cook on "low" for 4-6 hours, or until rice kernels are fully opened and rice is tender. Avoid over-cooking, and if rice becomes too dry, add in a little more vegetable broth. Makes 6-8 servings.

Rich and Velvety Mac and Cheese

Ingredients:

1 pound package (16 ounces) elbow macaroni (or other small shaped pasta)

1 stick of butter (unsalted - regular or vegan)

1 cup milk (regular or non-dairy)

1 can (12 ounces) evaporated milk

4 cups of shredded Colby Jack cheese (Sharp Cheddar cheese works well too)

1/2 teaspoon ground black pepper

1/2 teaspoon sea salt

1/2 teaspoon ground paprika

Cook the pasta according to package direction to al dente'. Rinse and drain thoroughly. Combine the cooked pasta along with all of the remaining ingredients in a large mixing bowl and toss until all ingredients are evenly blended.

Use butter or oil to grease the bottom and sides of your slow cooker. Transfer the mac and cheese mixture into your prepared slow cooker and cook on "low" for 4 hours. Taste and adjust seasonings as desired before serving. Makes 4-6 servings.

Zesty Refried Beans

Ingredients:

3 cups pinto beans (dry measurement)

2 cups diced yellow onion

4 fresh garlic cloves (minced)

1 whole jalapeno pepper (seeded and finely diced - more or less to heat preference)

1 teaspoon ground cumin

1/2 teaspoon ground black pepper

7 cups of vegetable broth

Soak the pinto beans overnight. The next day, drain, rinse and drain again.

Combine the soaked, drained beans along with all of the remaining ingredients in your slow cooker. Stir well to evenly blend and cook on "low" for 8-9 hours. Ladle out 1 cup of the liquid and reserve. Next, drain the bean mixture in a colander to remove the remaining liquid and return bean mixture to your slow cooker. Add in 1/2 cup of the reserved liquid and using a stick immersion blender, puree beans until smooth. If beans are too thick, add in more of the remaining reserved liquid to reach desired consistency. If you don't have a stick immersion blender, you can puree the beans in a food processor or even use a potato masher. You can use your zesty refried beans for burritos, tacos, Mexican casserole, to make dips and more. Makes 5-6 cups. * If you only need 1-2 cups, the refried beans freeze well, so you can put extras in an airtight, freezer-safe ziploc bag for future use.

Sweet Roasted Autumn Harvest Medley

Ingredients:

1 large butternut squash (about 2-1/2 to 3 pounds worth - peeled and cubed)

4 red variety apples (peeled and diced)

3/4 cup dried cranberries

2 tablespoons raw honey

2 teaspoons ground cinnamon

1 teaspoon ground nutmeg

drizzle of balsamic vinegar

drizzle of pure maple syrup

1/4 cup finely chopped nuts (walnuts or pecans)

Lightly grease the bottom and sides of your slow cooker with butter or oil. Combine all of the ingredients EXCEPT the balsamic vinegar, maple syrup and chopped nuts into your prepared slow cooker. Stir well to blend and cook on "low" for 8 hours, stirring every few hours. Stir in the balsamic vinegar (just a drizzle), maple syrup (just a drizzle) and the chopped nuts during the last 30 minutes of cooking time. Makes about 8 servings.

Baked Potatoes

Ingredients:

6 golden russet potatoes (washed and pierced liberally with a fork)

sea salt

aluminum foil

After washing and piercing potatoes, liberally salt the outsides and wrap each one tightly in aluminum foil. Do NOT skip piercing the potatoes, otherwise they will EXPLODE. Arrange the foil wrapped potatoes in your slow cooker and cook on "low" for 6-8 hours. If your slow cooker allows room for more potatoes, you can add them, but you'll need to increase cooking time to 10-12 hours. Makes 6 servings.

Vegan Stuffing

Ingredients:

2-3 tablespoons olive oil

2 cups diced yellow onions

2 cups diced celery

12 ounces diced mushrooms (any variety)

12 cups of dried, cubed French bread (I use a large loaf of French bread from Sprouts bakery and let it dry out overnight out of it's paper wrapping)

1/3 cup fresh chopped parsley

1 teaspoon poultry seasoning blend (see below on how to make

your own)

1-1/2 teaspoon ground sage

1 teaspoon dried thyme

1/2 teaspoon ground marjoram

1/2 teaspoon ground black pepper

1/2 teaspoon sea salt

4 cups vegetable broth (more as needed)

Heat the olive oil in a skillet over medium heat. Add in the diced onion, celery and mushrooms and saute until onions become translucent, about 4 minutes. Transfer the sauteed vegetable mixture into a large mixing bowl and add in all of the remaining ingredients EXCEPT the vegetable broth. Stir to blend the ingredients and then slowly start adding in the vegetable broth to moisten the stuffing mixture (3-1/2 to 4 cups).

Lightly oil the bottom and sides of your slow cooker with olive oil before adding stuffing mixture. Cook on "high" for 30 minutes and then reduce slow cooker heat to "low" and cook for an additional 3-4 hours. If stuffing looks like it's becoming too dry, drizzle in some extra vegetable broth. Makes 8-10 servings.

* If you don't have poultry seasoning blend, here is a recipe to make your own.

Combine 2 teaspoons ground sage; 1-1/2 teaspoons ground thyme; 1 teaspoon ground marjoram; 3/4 teaspoon dried rosemary; 1/2 teaspoon ground nutmeg; 1/2 teaspoon ground black pepper in a shaker and mixing bowl and store in an airtight plastic bag or spice container.

Seasoned Zucchini

Ingredients:

6 large zucchini (washed thoroughly, but not peeled and then rough chopped)

1 cup tomato juice (preferably organic or fresh juiced)

2 vegetable bouillon cubes

3 fresh garlic cloves (minced)

2-3 teaspoons dried parsley

1/2 teaspoon dried oregano

1/2 teaspoon ground black pepper

2 tablespoons fine diced green onions

sea salt (to taste)

*all-purpose flour to thicken sauce, if desired

Combine the tomato juice, vegetable bouillon cubes, minced garlic, parsley, oregano and black pepper in a mixing bowl and whisk to thoroughly blend and break up the bouillon cubes as much as possible. Add in the rough chopped zucchini and toss to coat. Transfer the zucchini mixture into your slow cooker, give another stir to blend and cook on "low" for 6-7 hours. The sauce will thicken during cooking time, but if you would like to thicken it further, sprinkle in just a little all-purpose flour and stir to evenly blend at the end of the cooking time. Season the zucchini with sea salt to taste, along with any additional seasonings as desired, transfer into a serving bowl and sprinkle the diced green onions on top. Makes 6-8 servings as a side. You can also serve this on top of a scoop of fresh steamed rice for a main dish, which would yield you closer to 4 servings.

Layered Beans and Barley

Ingredients:

1 cup barley (dry measurement - long-cooking kind - do NOT use quick cooking barley)

1 yellow onion (diced)

3-4 fresh garlic cloves (minced)

1 large celery stalk (finely diced)

1/4 teaspoon crushed red pepper flakes (use 1/2 teaspoon if you desire more heat)

1 teaspoon sea salt

1/4 teaspoon ground black pepper

1 can (15 ounce) red kidney beans (rinsed and drained)

3 cups diced tomatoes

3-1/2 cups vegetable broth

2 large bay leaves

Evenly layer each of the ingredients in the order that they are listed into your slow cooker. When you are ready to add in the vegetable broth, pour it in slowly and zig zag across the top of all the layered ingredients. Do NOT stir. Cook on "low" for 6-8 hours. Remove the bay leaves and stir thoroughly. Add any additional sea salt or black pepper as desired and serve. Makes 6 servings as a side, or 4 servings if served over a scoop of fresh steamed rice as a main dish.

Southwest Style Pinto Beans

Ingredients:

1 pound bag of pinto beans (dry measurement)

2 green chiles (seeded and finely diced)

1 teaspoon smoky paprika

1 teaspoon ground cumin

1 teaspoon sea salt

1 teaspoon ground black pepper

Soak the pinto beans in water overnight. The next day, drain, rinse and drain again. Put the pre-soaked beans in your slow cooker and cover with enough fresh water to cover by about 2 inches. Cook on "low" for 8-10 hours, or "high" for 5-6 hours.

Drain the beans in a colander and return to your slow cooker. Stir in all of the remaining ingredients and cook on "low" for 30 minutes. Serve as a side dish, or as a filling ingredient for your Mexican-inspired dishes.

Easy Roasted Vegetables

Ingredients:

2 tablespoons olive oil

1 large onion (rough chopped)

pinch of raw sugar

pinch of sea salt

2-3 fresh garlic cloves (minced)

3 cups peeled, cubed potatoes

3 cups sliced carrots

3 cups chopped mushrooms (any variety)

2 cups vegetable broth

1/2 teaspoon dried oregano

1/2 teaspoon dried thyme

1/2 teaspoon sea salt

1/2 teaspoon ground black pepper

Heat the olive oil in a skillet over medium heat. Add in the onions and stir in-frequently while they cook for about 5-7 minutes. Add in a pinch of sea salt and a pinch of raw sugar, stir to coat the onions and continue cooking until they begin to caramelize.

Transfer the caramelized onions into your slow cooker along with all of the remaining ingredients. Stir well to blend and cook on "low" for 8-9 hours. If mixture becomes too dry, you can drizzle in a little extra vegetable broth or water. Taste and adjust seasoning as desired before serving. Makes 6-8 servings as a side, or 4 servings if served over a scoop of fresh steamed rice or grains as a main dish.

Spanish Brown Rice

Ingredients:

3/4 cup brown rice (dry measurement - do not use quick cooking variety)

1-1/2 cups vegetable broth

1 yellow onion (diced)

3 fresh garlic cloves (minced)

1 green bell pepper (seeded and finely diced)

4 Roma tomatoes (finely diced)

1 can (15 ounce) plain tomato sauce

2 tablespoons of your favorite salsa

2 teaspoons vegetarian Worchestershire sauce (I use Wizards or Annies brands)

2 teaspoons chili powder

pinch of black pepper

Combine all of the ingredients into your slow cooker. Stir well to blend and cook on "low" for 6-8 hours. You want the rice to be tender, but try to avoid overcooking otherwise the rice will dry out. Makes 4-6 servings.

Curried Chickpeas with Vegetables

Ingredients:

4 tablespoons olive oil

2 yellow onions (diced)

6 fresh garlic cloves (minced)

4 large carrots (thinly sliced)

4 tablespoons curry powder

2 teaspoons ground coriander

1/2 teaspoon cayenne powder

4 large golden russet potatoes (peeled and cubed)

1 pound of green beans (ends trimmed and rough chopped)

3 cups diced tomatoes

2 cans (15 ounces each) chickpeas (rinsed and drained)

4 cups vegetable broth

1 cup green peas

1 can (14 ounce) coconut milk

sea salt and black pepper (to taste)

Heat the olive oil in a skillet over medium heat. Add in the diced onions and saute until onions become translucent, about 4 minutes. Add in the minced garlic and stir continuously until fragrant, about 30-60 seconds. Add in the sliced carrots, curry powder, coriander and cayenne powder and toss well to evenly coat while cooking for an additional 2-3 minutes.

Transfer the sauteed vegetable mixture into your slow cooker along with all of the remaining ingredients EXCEPT the peas and coconut milk. Stir well to blend and cook on "low" for 6-8 hours. Stir in the green peas and coconut milk during the final 30 minutes of cooking time. Taste and adjust seasonings as desired before serving. Makes 8 servings as a side dish, or 4-6 servings as a main dish when served over a scoop of fresh steamed rice.

Barley Medley

Ingredients:

3 tablespoons olive oil

6 large carrots (thinly sliced)

8 ounces of diced mushrooms (any variety)

2 cups barley (dry measurement - do NOT use quick-cooking barley)

4 cups (32 ounces) vegetable broth

2-3 teaspoons of table blend seasoning

1/2 teaspoon garlic powder

1/2 teaspoon sea salt

1 tablespoon Braggs liquid aminos (may use Tamari or regular soy sauce)

1/2 cup fine diced green onions

* fresh chopped parsley for garnish

Heat the olive oil in a skillet over medium heat. Add in the carrots and mushrooms and stir frequently while cooking for 4-5 minutes. Transfer the sauteed vegetable mixture into your slow cooker along with all of the remaining ingredients EXCEPT the diced green onions. Stir well to blend and cook on "low" for 4-5 hours. Taste and adjust seasonings as desired and serve with a sprinkle of fresh chopped parsley. Makes 6 servings.

Zesty Southwest Red Beans

Ingredients:

1 pound (16 ounces) red kidney beans (dry measurement)

3 tablespoons olive oil

1 large yellow onion (diced)

4-5 fresh garlic cloves (minced)

4 cups (32 ounces) vegetables broth

2 cups diced tomatoes

2 teaspoons ground cumin

1-1/2 teaspoons sea salt

1 teaspoon crushed red pepper flakes

* fresh chopped cilantro and lime wedges for garnish

Heat the olive oil in a skillet over medium heat. Add in the diced onion and saute until onions become translucent, about 4 minutes. Add in the minced garlic and stir continuously until fragrant, about 30-60 seconds. Transfer the onion-garlic mixture into your slow cooker along with all of the remaining ingredients. Stir well to blend and cook on "low" for 10-12 hours OR cook on "high" for 2 hours - reduce heat to "low" and cook on "low" for 8 hours. Taste and adjust seasonings as desired before serving with the fresh chopped cilantro and lime wedges. Makes 8 servings.

Spiced Sweet Potatoes and Apples

Ingredients:

5 large sweet potatoes (peeled and cubed)

2 large red variety apples (peeled and diced)

1/4 cup pure maple syrup

2 heaping tablespoons brown sugar

2 tablespoon melted butter (regular or vegan)

1/2 teaspoon sea salt

1/4 teaspoon ground black pepper

1/4 teaspoon ground cinnamon

1/4 teaspoon ground nutmeg

Whisk together the maple syrup, brown sugar, melted butter and seasonings in a large mixing bowl. Once blended, add in the cubed sweet potatoes and diced apples and toss to evenly coat and blend. Transfer mixture into your slow cooker and cook on "low" for 4-6 hours. Taste and adjust seasonings as desired before serving. Makes 6 servings.

Cheesy Potatoes with Veggies

Ingredients:

5 large golden russet potatoes (peeled and cubed or thinly sliced)

3 tablespoons olive oil

1 yellow onion (diced)

3 fresh garlic cloves (minced)

6 tablespoons of butter (cut into small pieces)

1 teaspoon sea salt

1 teaspoon ground black pepper

1-1/2 cups of diced veggies of your choice (green beans, mushrooms, bell peppers, asparagus, etc.)

1 cup of shredded sharp Cheddar cheese

Heat the olive oil in a skillet over medium heat. Add in the diced onions and saute until onions become translucent, about 4 minutes. Add in the minced garlic and stir continuously until fragrant, about 30-60 seconds. Transfer the sauteed onion-garlic mixture into your slow cooker along with all of the remaining ingredients EXCEPT the diced veggies and shredded cheese. Stir well to blend and cook on "low" for 6-8 hours. Stir in the diced veggies and shredded cheese during the last 1 hour of cooking time. Taste and adjust seasonings as desired before serving. Makes 6 servings.

Pineapple Barbeque Baked Beans

Ingredients:

2 cans (15 ounces each) pinto beans (rinsed and drained)

2/3 cup diced pineapple (or one 8 ounce can of diced pineapple, well drained)

1 yellow onion (diced)

3 fresh garlic cloves (minced)

1/2-3/4 cup of your favorite barbeque sauce

2 tablespoons real maple syrup

1 tablespoon Braggs liquid aminos (may also use Tamari or regular soy sauce)

sea salt and black pepper (to taste)

* fresh chopped cilantro for garnish (optional)

Combine all of the ingredients into your slow cooker. Stir well to blend and cook on "low" for 6-8 hours. Taste and adjust seasonings as desired before serving with a sprinkle of fresh chopped cilantro (optional). Makes 6 servings.

Spicy Picante Style Lentil and Tomatoes

Ingredients:

3 tablespoons olive oil

1 large yellow onion (diced)

6-7 fresh garlic cloves (minced)

2 green chiles (seeded and diced)

1/2 cup lentils (dry measurement - rinse and drain thoroughly before using)

5 cups diced tomatoes

2 teaspoons raw sugar

1 teaspoon ground cumin

1 cup picante sauce (medium or hot)

1/2 teaspoon ground black pepper

Heat the olive oil in a skillet over medium heat. Add in the diced onion and saute until onion becomes translucent, about 4 minutes. Add in the minced garlic and diced green chiles and stir continuously until fragrant, about 30-60 seconds. Transfer the sauteed onion-garlic mixture into your slow cooker along with all of the remaining ingredients. Stir well to blend and cook on "low" for 6-8 hours until lentils are very tender. Taste and adjust seasonings as desired. Makes 8 servings.

Sweet and Savory Cabbage

Ingredients:

1 cup natural apple juice (no sugar added)

1/2 cup vegetable broth

3 tablespoons brown mustard

1/2 teaspoon sea salt

1/4 teaspoon ground black pepper

1 medium-sized head of green cabbage (coarsely chopped)

2 large apples (peeled and diced)

1 large yellow onion (rough chopped)

Liberally grease the bottom and sides of your slow cooker with butter or oil. In a large mixing bowl, whisk together the apple juice, vegetable broth, brown mustard, sea salt and black pepper until well blended. Add in the cabbage, apples and onions and toss to evenly coat all ingredients. Transfer mixture into your prepared slow cooker and cook on "low" for 6-8 hours, stirring well every 2-3 hours. Taste and adjust sea salt and black pepper as desired before serving. Makes 6-8 servings.

Chapter 7 –
Slow Cooker Recipes: Desserts

Red and Blue Berry Cobbler

Ingredients:

1 cup all-purpose flour

3 tablespoons raw sugar

1 teaspoon aluminum-free baking powder

1/4 teaspoon ground cinnamon

1 large egg (beaten)

1/4 cup milk (regular or non-dairy)

2 tablespoons light oil (such as grapeseed, safflower, sunflower, etc.)

pinch of sea salt

(topping)

1 cup raw sugar

1/4 cup all-purpose flour

pinch of sea salt

2 cups raspberries

2 cups blueberries

1/2 tablespoon fresh squeezed lemon juice

(* It's ok to use frozen berries, but make sure to thaw and dry off any excess water moisture with paper towels first.)

In a mixing bowl, sift together the first 4 ingredients. In a separate mixing bowl, whisk together the egg, milk, oil and pinch of sea salt. Slowly pour the wet ingredient mixture into the bowl with the dry ingredient mixture and stir until all ingredients are moistened and evenly blended, without over-mixing. Pour mixture into bottom of your slow cooker.

In a separate mixing bowl, whisk together the 1 cup of raw sugar, 1/4 of flour and pinch of sea salt. Add in the raspberries, blueberries and lemon juice, and toss gently until all of the berries are evenly coated and well combined. Spoon the berry mixture on top of the batter mixture in your slow cooker and cook on "low" for about 2-1/2 hours, or until the batter is cooked through. Serve as-is, or with a scoop of non-dairy ice-cream for a delicious treat. Makes 4-6 servings.

Spruced Up Coconut Rice Pudding

Ingredients:

2 cans (14 ounce each) coconut milk

2 cups unsweetened coconut milk (you may also use rice or almond milk)

1 cup basmati rice (dry measurement)

1/2-1 cup water (to desired consistency)

1/2 tablespoon pure vanilla extract

1 teaspoon ground cinnamon

1/2 teaspoon ground nutmeg

1 cup raisins (dark or golden)

1/2 cup finely chopped pecans

1/2 cup finely shredded coconut (unsweetened)

1/2 cup raw honey (may also use raw agave nectar)

Add all the ingredients EXCEPT for the raisins, pecans, shredded coconut and raw honey into your slow cooker. Stir well for 1-2 minutes to blend. Cook on "low" for 4 hours. After 4 hours, stir in the raisins, chopped pecans and shredded coconut and cook for a final 15 minutes. Spoon into individual serving bowls and drizzle each with a little of the raw honey (or raw agave nectar). Makes 8 servings.

Caramel Glazed Pears

Ingredients:

6 Bosc pears (peeled, cored and cut into halves)

1-1/2 cups packed brown sugar

3 tablespoons stick butter (regular or vegan - cut into small pieces)

1 tablespoon fresh grated ginger

In a large mixing bowl, stir together the brown sugar, butter pieces and grated ginger using a fork to help "cut" in the butter. Add in your prepped pears and gently toss to evenly coat the pears. Transfer the pears, along with the glaze mixture, into your slow cooker and cook on "low" for 4 hours, or until the pears are tender and easily pierced with the tip of a knife. You can alternately cook the pears on "high" for about 2 hours. Spoon 2 pear halves into individual serving bowls and spoon some of the caramel glaze across the top. Serve as-is or with a scoop of non-dairy ice-cream. Makes 6 servings.

Nutty Chocolate on Chocolate Brownies

(line the bottom of your slow cooker with parchment paper and then brush a thin layer of oil on top - I use coconut oil)

Ingredients:

1-1/4 cups all-purpose flour

1/4 cup cocoa powder (unsweetened)

3/4 teaspoon aluminum-free baking powder

1/2 teaspoon sea salt

1 stick of butter (unsalted)

8 ounces bittersweet baking chocolate (rough chopped)

1 cup semi-sweet chocolate chips

1 cup raw sugar

3 large eggs (well beaten)

1 cup finely chopped nuts (walnuts, pecans, almonds)

Sift the flour, cocoa powder, baking powder and sea salt together in a mixing bowl and set aside.

Using a double boiler or a heat-safe bowl over a pot of boiling water, add in the stick of butter, baking chocolate and chocolate chips, and stir continuously until butter and chocolate are fully melted. Once the chocolate is fully melted, whisk in the raw sugar and beaten eggs. Slowly pour the melted chocolate mixture into the bowl with the dry ingredient mixture and stir until all ingredients are moistened and well blended. Lastly, stir in the chopped nuts and then carefully pour batter into your prepared slow cooker.

Cook on "low" for 4 hours, removing lid during the last 30 minutes of cooking time. Carefully remove the cooked brownies by holding onto the parchment paper, and once you have it on a flat surface, let the brownies rest for 5-7 minutes before inverting onto a wire rack to finish cooling. I recommend letting the brownies cool for at least 2-3 hours before cutting and serving. The brownies will continue setting and firming up as they cool, which is why you don't want to cut them too early. If the brownies are sticking to the parchment paper, carefully run a knife between the two to loosen. Makes approximately 12 cut pieces.

Apple Pie Crisp

Ingredients:

6 heaping cups of peeled, diced apples (any variety, but I tend to prefer the sweeter varieties for this dish)

2 tablespoons fresh squeezed lemon juice

6 tablespoons butter (divided)

1 tablespoon cornstarch (may also use arrowroot powder or tapioca starch)

2 tablespoon apple pie spice (divided)

1 cup packed brown sugar (divided)

1/3 cup finely chopped nuts (walnuts or pecans work best)

3/4 cup all-purpose flour

pinch of sea salt

dusting of ground cinnamon

Combine the diced apples, lemon juice and 2 tablespoons of the butter in a mixing bowl and stir well until apples are evenly coated. In a small mixing bowl, whisk together the cornstarch, 1 tablespoon of the apple pie spice and 1/4 cup of the brown sugar until well combined. Add the mixture into the bowl with the apples and again stir to evenly coat the apples. Pour the apple mixture into your slow cooker and evenly sprinkle the chopped walnuts across the top.

In a separate mixing bowl, stir together the flour, the remaining 3/4 cup of brown sugar, the remaining 1 tablespoon of apple pie spice and the remaining 4 tablespoons of butter, using a fork or pastry cutter to "cut" in the butter. Keep mixing until mixture resembles wet sand. Crumble the mixture evenly across the top of the ingredients already in the slow cooker and sprinkle a light dusting of ground cinnamon on top. Cook on "low" for 4-5 hours. Serve as-is or with a scoop of non-dairy ice-cream. Makes 6 servings.

Chocolate Lava Cake

Ingredients:

1 cup all-purpose flour

2 teaspoons aluminum-free baking powder

6 tablespoons butter (regular or vegan)

2 ounces semi-sweet chocolate chips

1 cup raw sugar (divided)

1/3 cup PLUS 3 tablespoons Dutch processed cocoa powder

1 tablespoon pure vanilla extract

1/4 teaspoon sea salt

1/3 cup plain milk (regular or non-dairy)

1 large egg yolk

1/3 cup packed brown sugar

1-1/2 cups hot water (but not boiling)

Lightly grease the bottom and sides of your slow cooker with butter or oil.

Sift together the flour and baking powder into a large mixing bowl and set aside.

In a double boiler or in a heat-safe bowl over a bowl of simmering water, melt the chocolate chips and butter while stirring continuously. Once melted, stir in 2/3 cup of the raw sugar and 3 tablespoons of the Dutch cocoa until fully dissolved. Once dissolved, stir in the vanilla extract, sea salt, milk and egg yolk until mixture is well blended and smooth. Slowly pour the chocolate mixture into the bowl with the flour mixture and stir until flour is fully combined and mixture is thoroughly blended. Evenly pour the chocolate lava mixture into the bottom of your prepared slow cooker.

In a mixing bowl, stir together the remaining 1/3 cup of raw sugar, the remaining 1/3 cup of Dutch cocoa, the 1/3 cup brown sugar and 1-1/2 cups of hot water until well blended and creamy smooth. All of the sugar should be fully dissolved. Slowly pour the mixture across the top of the other layer in your slow cooker WITHOUT stirring. Cook on "high" for 1-1/2 to 2-1/2 hours. Cake will be very moist looking and should be floating on a layer of molten chocolate. You will know the cake is ready when nearly all of the cake is set and the edges begin to pull away from the sides of your slow cooker. Turn off slow cooker and remove the lid. Let cake sit for 30-40 minutes before serving as-is or with a scoop of non-dairy ice-cream. Makes 6 servings.

Easy Rum Bread Pudding

Ingredients:

8 cups of cubed French or Sourdough bread (preferably slightly old and crusty)

5 large eggs

4 cups plain milk (regular or non-dairy)

1 tablespoon pure vanilla extract

3 tablespoons rum (light or dark)

3/4 cup raw sugar

1 tablespoon ground cinnamon

pinch of sea salt

*optional add-ins: raisins; dried cranberries; chopped nuts; toasted, shredded coconut

Whisk the eggs in a large mixing bowl until well beaten. Stir in the milk, vanilla extract, rum, raw sugar, ground cinnamon and sea salt until well blended. Add in the cubed bread and toss until evenly coated. Let the mixture sit for 20-30 minutes to allow the bread to absorb all of the liquid, occasionally pressing on the bread cubes to assist in the absorption process.

Liberally grease the bottom and sides of your slow cooker with butter. Transfer the bread pudding mixture into your slow cooker and cook on "low" for 5-7 hours. If you'll be using any of the optional add-in ingredients, stir them in, in desired quantity about midway through the cooking time. If pudding becomes too dry during the cooking process, drizzle in a little extra milk to keep moist. Makes about 8 servings.

Spiced Applesauce

Ingredients:

10 large red apples (peeled and cubed)

2 tablespoons pure maple syrup

2-3 teaspoons fresh squeezed lemon juice

1-1/2 teaspoons ground cinnamon

1/2 teaspoon ground cloves

1/2 teaspoon ground cardamom

tiny pinch of ground ginger

Whisk together all of the ingredients EXCEPT the apple cubes in the bottom of your slow cooker until well blended. Add in the apple cubes and toss well to evenly coat. Cook on "high" for 3-4 hours, or "low" for 7-8 hours. To finish to desired consistency you can either use a potato masher, or transfer the mixture into a blender or food processor to achieve desired consistency. I personally like this a little on the chunky side, so I prefer to use a potato masher. Serve as-is or with a scoop of non-dairy ice-cream for a delicious and healthy treat. Makes 4-6 servings.

Coconut, Apricot and Pecan Rice Pudding

Ingredients:

1 cup arborio rice (dry measurement)

2-1/2 cups plain milk (regular or non-dairy)

1 can (14 ounce) coconut milk

1/2 cup raw sugar

pinch of sea salt

1 small cinnamon stick

1 cup finely chopped dried apricots

1/4 cup finely chopped pecans

Lightly oil the bottom and sides of your slow cooker with coconut oil or butter. Combine the rice, milk, coconut milk, raw sugar and sea salt in your slow cooker and stir well to blend. Drop in the cinnamon stick and cook on "low" for 5-6 hours or "high" for 2-1/2 hours, or until rice is tender and mixture has thickened. Discard the cinnamon stick and stir in the chopped apricots and pecans. Turn off heat and let the pudding rest for 15 minutes before serving. Makes 4-6 servings.

Chocolate Cake

Ingredients:

1-3/4 cup flour (all-purpose)

2 cups raw sugar

3/4 cup cocoa powder (unsweetened)

1-1/2 teaspoons aluminum-free baking powder

1-1/2 teaspoons baking soda

1 teaspoon sea salt

2 large eggs

1 cup milk (regular or non-dairy)

1/2 cup vegetable oil

2 teaspoons pure vanilla extract

1 cup of very hot water

* optional toppings: powdered sugar; warm chocolate sauce; fresh fruit; scoop of non-dairy ice-cream, etc.

Liberally grease the bottom and sides of your slow cooker with butter or oil.

In a mixing bowl, whisk together the flour, raw sugar, cocoa powder, baking powder, baking soda and sea salt. In a separate mixing bowl, whisk together the eggs, milk, oil and vanilla extract until well blended. Continue whisking while slowly pouring in the hot water. Pour the wet ingredient mixture into the bowl with the dry ingredient mixture and stir until all ingredients are well moistened and evenly blended, but do not over-mix.

Pour batter into your prepared slow cooker and cook on "low" for 3 to 3-1/2 hours, or until the cake has no wet spots on top and has pulled away from the sides of the slow cooker. Turn off the slow cooker and let the cake rest for 30-45 minutes before cutting and serving with an optional suggested topping. Makes 6-8 servings.

Chocolate Cherry Bread Pudding

Ingredients:

4 large eggs

1-3/4 cups milk (regular or non-dairy)

1/3 cup cocoa powder (unsweetened)

1/2 cup raw sugar

1/2 cup mini chocolate chips

1/2 cup dried cherries (rough chopped - may substitute with dried cranberries)

1/2 teaspoon pure vanilla extract

10 large slices of STALE French bread (cubed)

Lightly grease the bottom and sides of your slow cooker with butter or oil.

In a mixing bowl, whisk the eggs until well beaten. Stir in all of the remaining ingredients EXCEPT the bread until all ingredients are well blended. Add in the cubed bread and toss to evenly coat. Let the mixture sit for about 20 minutes to allow the bread to absorb the liquid. Transfer mixture into your slow cooker and cook on "low" for 3-4 hours, or until set. Serve as-is or with a dusting of powdered sugar. Makes 4-6 servings.

Amaretto Spiked Fruit Compote

Ingredients:

4 large pears (peeled and rough chopped)

4 large peaches (rough chopped)

2 cups diced pineapple

3/4 cup Amaretto liqueur

1/2 cup packed brown sugar

1 vanilla bean

* toasted shredded coconut (optional)

** non-dairy ice-cream, cake or brownie to serve compote over

Combine all of the ingredients into your slow cooker. Stir gently to combine and cook on "low" for 2-1/2 to 3 hours. Remove the vanilla bean and serve over non-dairy ice-cream, cake or brownie with an optional garnish of toasted, shredded coconut. May also just serve as-is with some shredded coconut. Makes 4-6 servings.

Nut and Raisin Stuffed Apples

Ingredients:

6 large red variety apples (cored)

1/2 cup water

1/2 cup packed brown sugar

1 teaspoon ground cinnamon

pinch of nutmeg

2 tablespoons of finely chopped nuts (walnuts or pecans)

2 tablespoons raisins (dark or golden)

3 tablespoons butter

In a mixing bowl, stir together the brown sugar, cinnamon, nutmeg, chopped nuts and raisins until well combined. Pour the water into your slow cooker. Evenly stuff the 6 cored apples with the nut and raisin mixture and place in the water in your slow cooker. Dot 1/2 tablespoon of butter onto the top of each of the 6 stuffed apples and cook on "low" for 6-8 hours. Serve as-is or with a scoop of non-dairy ice-cream for a delicious and healthy dessert. Makes 6 servings.

Pumpkin, Raisin and Walnut Bread Pudding

Ingredients:

6 large eggs

3 to 3-1/2 cups plain milk (regular or non-dairy)

1 cup packed brown sugar

1 can (15 ounce) pumpkin puree (I love Farmer's Market Organic Pumpkin Puree)

1-1/2 cups finely chopped walnuts

1 cup dark raisins (give a rough chop)

1 tablespoon pure vanilla extract

1 teaspoon ground cinnamon

1/2 teaspoon ground nutmeg

1/2 teaspoon ground ginger

1/4 teaspoon ground cardamom

pinch of sea salt

10 cups of cubed STALE sourdough or French bread

Lightly grease bottom and sides of your slow cooker with butter or oil.

In a large mixing bowl, whisk the eggs until well beaten. Stir in all of the remaining ingredients EXCEPT the cubed bread until well blended. Add in the cubed, stale bread and toss to evenly coat. Let the mixture sit for about 20 minutes to allow the bread to absorb all the liquid. Transfer mixture into your prepared slow cooker and cook on "low" for 4-6 hours. Turn off slow cooker, remove lid and let the pudding rest for 15-20 minutes before serving as-is or with a dollop of fresh whipped cream. Makes 8-10 servings.

Candied Pecans

Ingredients:

1-1/2 teaspoons ground cinnamon

1/4 teaspoon ground ginger

1/4 teaspoon ground allspice

1/2 cup melted butter

1 pound (16 ounces) pecan halves

1/2 cup powdered sugar

Whisk together the cinnamon, ginger and allspice in a large mixing bowl and then set aside.

In a separate mixing bowl, toss together the melted butter and pecan halves. Add in the powdered sugar and toss to evenly coat and blend. Transfer the coated pecans into your slow cooker and cook on "high" for 15 minutes. Immediately reduce heat to "low" and cook for an additional 2 hours, or until pecans become lightly crisped and glazed. Carefully transfer the hot nuts into the mixing bowl with the combined spices and toss to evenly coat. Allow the pecans to cool COMPLETELY before serving. The sweet spice mixture will continue to set onto the pecans as they cool. Makes 1 pound of candied pecans.

Spiced Scone Pudding

Ingredients:

3 large eggs

2/3 cup unsulphured blackstrap molasses

2 tablespoons butter (softened to room temperature)

1/2 teaspoon ground cinnamon

1/2 teaspoon ground ginger

1/4 teaspoon ground mace

3 cups plain milk (regular or non-dairy)

1/2 cup cornmeal (coarse-grind)

1/2 teaspoon sea salt

2/3 cup rough chopped dark raisins

Oil the bottom and sides of your slow cooker with butter or oil.

In a mixing bowl, whisk the eggs until well beaten. Add in the molasses, softened butter, cinnamon, ginger and mace and whisk until all ingredients are well blended and set aside.

In a saucepan, scald the milk over medium-high heat (small bubbles appear along the edge of the pan). Stir in the cornmeal and sea salt and immediately decrease the heat to low. Stir continuously while cooking for 10 minutes, until the mixture thickens. Remove from heat and slowly add the spiced egg mixture into the hot milk-cornmeal mixture while whisking continuously until smooth. Stir in the raisins and transfer mixture into your prepared slow cooker. Cook on "low" for 6-8 hours, until pudding is set. Serve as-is, or with a dusting of powdered sugar, a dollop of fresh whipped cream, or a scoop of non-dairy ice-cream. Makes 6 servings.

Tropical Banana Rum Medley

Ingredients:

1/2 cup packed brown sugar

3 tablespoons butter (softened to room temperature)

1/4 cup coconut milk (from a can, and I recommend using full-fat)

1/4 cup dark rum

4 ripe bananas (cut into 1/2 inch slices)

1 cup diced pineapple (if using canned, be sure to thoroughly drain first)

1/4 teaspoon ground cinnamon

pinch of nutmeg

* non-dairy ice-cream, pound cake or angel food cake to serve medley over

Lightly oil the bottom and sides of your slow cooker with butter or coconut oil. (Don't use olive or vegetable oil, as this will alter the taste.) Add the brown sugar, softened butter, coconut milk and dark rum into your prepared slow cooker and stir to blend. Cook on "low" for 1 hour. Give the mixture a good whisking to keep smooth. Stir in the sliced bananas, diced pineapple, cinnamon and nutmeg and cook on "low" for an additional 15 minutes. Serve immediately over some non-dairy ice-cream, pound cake or angel food cake for a delicious taste of the islands dessert. Makes 6 servings.

Dressed Up Caramel Baked Pears

Ingredients:

6 large, just ripe pears (peeled and cored - make sure they are not overripe)

1 cup caramel ice-cream topping

1/3 cup real maple syrup

1/2 cup chopped raisin (dark or golden)

1/4 cup chopped dried cranberries

1 teaspoon of fresh grated lemon peel

Lightly grease the bottom and sides of your slow cooker with coconut oil or butter. Arrange the cored pears into your prepared slow cooker. (If all pears do not fit in bottom of cooker, place remaining pears suspended between 2 others in cooker.)

In a mixing bowl, stir together the caramel topping and maple syrup and evenly drizzle over pears. Cook on "High" for 2-1/2 to 3-1/2 hours. Using a slotted spoon, carefully transfer the baked pears onto a serving platter (or individual serving plates or bowls) and drizzle some of the reserved caramel-maple topping across the top of each one.

Stir together the chopped raisins, chopped dried cranberries and grated lemon peel in a bowl and evenly sprinkle some of the topping across the top of each pear. Serve as-is or with a scoop of non-dairy ice-cream. Makes 6 servings.

Cinnamon-Raisin Bread and Chocolate Chip Pudding

Ingredients:

3 large eggs

1 cup milk (regular or non-dairy)

1 cup heavy

1/4 cup melted butter (regular or vegan)

1/2 cup packed brown sugar

1 teaspoon pure vanilla extract

1/2 teaspoon ground nutmeg

1 loaf of STALE cinnamon raisin bread (cubed)

1/2 cup mini chocolate chips

1/2 cup finely chopped nuts (pecans or walnuts)

Lightly grease the bottom and sides of your slow cooker with butter or coconut oil

In a large mixing bowl, whisk the eggs until well beaten. Once beaten, whisk in the milk, heavy cream, melted butter, brown sugar, vanilla extract and nutmeg until all ingredients are well blended. Add in the stale, cubed cinnamon raisin bread and toss well to evenly coat. Let the mixture rest for 20-30 minutes to allow the liquid to be absorbed. Stir in the chocolate chips and chopped pecans, transfer mixture into your prepared slow cooker and cook on "low" for 2 to 2-1/2 hours, or until center is set. Turn off heat and let the pudding rest while still covered for another 30-40 minutes before serving. Makes 6 servings.

Spiced Apple Cake

Ingredients:

1-1/2 cups all-purpose flour

1/3 cup packed brown sugar

1 teaspoon baking soda

1-1/2 teaspoons ground cinnamon

1/2 teaspoon aluminum-free baking powder

1/4 teaspoon sea salt

1/4 teaspoon ground nutmeg

1/8 teaspoon ground cloves

1 large egg

1 cup natural applesauce (unsweetened)

1/3 cup buttermilk

1/4 cup melted butter

1 tablespoon pure vanilla extract

1 cup dried apple slices (unsweetened and chopped)

Lightly oil the bottom and sides of your slow cooker with oil. Line slow cooker with parchment paper by taking two long strips and crossing (like a plus sign) in either direction, and long enough to allow you to lift and remove cake after cooking time. Brush another light coat of oil on top of the parchment paper, as well.

In a mixing bowl, thoroughly whisk together the flour, brown sugar, baking soda, cinnamon, baking powder, sea salt, nutmeg and cloves until well combined. In a separate mixing bowl, whisk the egg until well beaten. Add in the applesauce, buttermilk, melted butter and vanilla extract and continue whisking until mixture is smooth and well blended. Slowly pour the wet ingredient mixture into the bowl with the dry ingredient mixture and stir until all ingredients are moistened and well blended but without over-mixing. Fold in the chopped dried apples and pour batter into your prepared slow cooker. Cook on "high" for about 1-1/2 hours, or until caked has risen and toothpick comes out clean from center.

Turn off slow cooker and let the cake rest for 15 minutes before carefully lifting out using the edges of the parchment paper. If parchment paper is sticking, you can also just cut the cake while still in the slow cooker. Serve as-is or with a dusting of powdered sugar, a dollop of fresh whipped cream or a scoop of non-dairy ice-cream. Makes 6-8 servings.

Decadent Tiramisu Bread Pudding

Ingredients:

1/2 cup water

1-1/2 tablespoons instant espresso granules

1/3 cup raw sugar

2 tablespoons Kahlua liqueur

2 cups milk (regular or non-dairy - divided)

2 large eggs (well beaten)

8 heaping cups of STALE cubed French bread

1/3 cup mascarpone cheese

1 teaspoon pure vanilla extract

2 teaspoons unsweetened cocoa powder (or more, as needed)

Lightly oil the bottom and sides of your slow cooker with coconut oil.

Combine the water, espresso granules and raw sugar in a saucepan and whisk continuously while bringing to a boil over medium heat. Allow mixture to boil for 1 minute, then remove from heat and stir in the Kahlua liqueur.

In a large mixing bowl, whisk together 1-3/4 cups of the milk and beaten eggs until well blended. Pour in the hot espresso mixture and whisk to blend. Add in the cubed French bread and toss well to evenly coat. Let mixture rest for about 20 minutes to allow liquid to be absorbed into bread. Transfer mixture into your prepared slow cooker and cook on "low" for 2 to 2-1/2 hours, or until set. Turn off slow cooker and let mixture rest for 15 minutes.

In a mixing bowl, stir together the remaining 1/4 cup milk, mascarpone cheese and vanilla extract until creamy and well blended. To serve, spoon some of the pudding into individual serving bowls, evenly spoon a little bit of the mascarpone mixture on top of each serving and dust with some of the cocoa powder. Makes 8 servings.

Coconut Apple Crumble

Ingredients:

4 cups of peeled, diced green variety apples

1/2 cup finely shredded coconut

1/3 cup packed brown sugar

1 tablespoon all-purpose flour

1/2 teaspoon ground cinnamon

1/2 cup caramel ice-cream topping

1/2 cup rolled oats

1/3 cup all-purpose flour

1/4 teaspoon sea salt

4 tablespoons cold butter (cut into small pieces)

Lightly grease the bottom and sides of your slow cooker with butter.

In a mixing bowl, toss together the diced apples, shredded coconut, brown sugar, 1 tablespoon flour and cinnamon until evenly coated and well combined. Transfer mixture into your prepared slow cooker and evenly drizzle the caramel topping across the top.

In a mixing bowl, stir together the rolled oats, 1/3 cup flour, sea salt and butter, using a fork or pastry cutter to "cut" in the butter. Crumble mixture should resemble wet sand. Evenly sprinkle the crumble mixture across the top and cook on "high" for about 3 hours, or "low" for about 5-6 hours. Serve as-is, or with a dollop of fresh whipped cream or non-dairy ice-cream. Makes 4 servings.

Anytime of the Year Pumpkin Pie Pudding

Ingredients:

4 large eggs

2 cans (15 ounces each) pumpkin puree

2 cans (12 ounces each) evaporated milk

1-1/2 cups raw sugar

1 cup vegan biscuit baking mix (may also use Bisquick)

4 tablespoons melted butter

5 teaspoons pumpkin pie spice

4 teaspoons pure vanilla extract

pinch of sea salt

Lightly grease the bottom and sides of your slow cooker with butter or oil.

In a mixing bowl, whisk the eggs until well beaten. Once the eggs are beaten, stir in all of the remaining ingredients until well blended. Transfer the mixture into your slow cooker and cook on "low" for 6-8 hours. Turn off heat and let pudding rest for 15 minutes before serving as-is or with a dollop of fresh whipped cream. Makes 8-10 servings.

Spiced Stewed Apples

Ingredients:

5 pound bag of green apples (peeled and rough chopped)

2 cups raw sugar

6 tablespoons cornstarch

5 tablespoons butter (regular or vegan - cut into small pieces)

2 teaspoons ground cinnamon

1/4 teaspoon ground nutmeg

pinch of sea salt

In a mixing bowl, stir together the raw sugar, cornstarch, butter pieces, cinnamon, nutmeg and sea salt until well blended. Add in the chopped apples and toss to evenly coat and blend all ingredients. Transfer mixture into your slow cooker and cook on "low" for 3-4 hours, stirring every hour if possible. Watch the mixture closely around the 3 hour mark, as you don't want to overcook the apples. Overcooking will turn the mixture into applesauce vs. stewed apples. So, this is another option if you do indeed want to make applesauce. Serve as-is, over spooned over a scoop of non-dairy ice-cream or a piece of cake or brownie. Makes 8 servings.

Amaretto Cherry Cobbler

Ingredients:

1 can (21 ounce) cherry pie filling (see below for how to make your own cherry pie filling)

1 cup all-purpose flour

1/3 cup raw sugar

1/4 cup melted butter (regular or vegan)

1/2 cup milk (regular or non-dairy)

1-1/2 teaspoons aluminum-free baking powder

1/2 teaspoon almond extract

1/4 teaspoon sea salt (use just a pinch if using salted butter)

2 teaspoons Amaretto liqueur

1 cup finely chopped nuts (walnuts or pecans - optional)

Lightly grease the bottom and sides of your slow cooker.

Evenly spread the cherry pie filling into the bottom of your slow cooker. In a mixing bowl, thoroughly stir together all of the remaining ingredients until evenly moistened and well blended. Batter should be very smooth. If batter is too moist, stir in a little extra flour to reach desired consistency. Evenly pour batter across top of cherry pie filling WITHOUT stirring. Cook on "low" for 3-5 hours, or until toothpick comes out clean from center. Turn off slow cooker and let the cobbler sit for 15 minutes before serving as-is or with a scoop of non-dairy ice-cream. Makes 6 servings.

* To makes your own cherry pie filling, place 4 cups of pitted cherries in a saucepan over medium-low heat and heat until cherries release their juices and come to a simmer, about 15 minutes. In a mixing bowl, stir together 1 cup raw sugar and 1/4 cup cornstarch and pour into the pan with the simmering cherries. Stir thoroughly and continuously until mixture thickens, about 2-3 minutes. Remove from heat and let cool. Your cherry pie filling is now ready to use.

Chapter 8 –
Slow Cooker Recipes:
Miscellaneous Mains

Lasagna with Vegetarian Meat Substitute

(lightly oil the bottom and sides of your slow cooker with olive oil)

Ingredients:

1 large jar (24 ounces) of your favorite marinara sauce (I use Amy's organic brand)

1-1/2 cups diced tomatoes

2 teaspoons Italian seasoning blend

3 fresh garlic cloves (minced)

1 package (8 ounces) no-boil lasagna noodles (divided)

1 container (15 ounces) ricotta cheese (warmed to room temperature - divided)

8-10 ounces shredded Mozzarella cheese (or shredded Italian cheese blend – divided)

1 bunch of baby spinach (hand torn – divided)

1 heaping cup of meatless veggie crumbles

In a mixing bowl, stir together the marinara sauce, diced tomatoes, Italian seasoning blend and minced garlic until well combined.

Spoon 1 cup of the marinara mixture into the bottom of your oiled slow cooker. Evenly arrange ¼ of the no-boil lasagna noodles across the sauce, carefully breaking and overlapping the pieces as necessary so that the bottom is completely covered.

Spoon about ¾ cup of the marinara mixture on top of the noodles, and then carefully spread 1/3 of the ricotta cheese across the top, followed by ½ of the hand torn baby spinach and 1/3 of the shredded cheese. Repeat layering two more times, but with the middle layer, replace the spinach with the entire 1 cup of veggie crumbles. The final layer should be the shredded cheese and topped with any remaining (or extra) marinara sauce. Cook on "low" for 3 hours, turn off heat and let the lasagna set for 10 minutes before serving. Makes 6-8 servings.

Southwest Style Stuffed Peppers
(lightly oil bottom and sides of your slow cooker)

Ingredients:

4 bell peppers, any variety (green, red, yellow, orange or yellow)

1 can (15 ounces) black beans (rinsed and drained)

1 cup of shredded Monterey Jack cheese

¾ cup of your favorite salsa

¼ cup diced onion

½ cup corn

1/3 cup (dry, uncooked measurement) long-grain, converted rice

1-1/4 teaspoons chili powder

½ teaspoon ground cumin

generous squeeze of fresh lime juice (about ½ - 1 whole lime)

Slice off the tops of the bell peppers and carefully scrape out the seeds and pith.

Combine all of the remaining ingredients in a mixing bowl and stir until well combined. Evenly spoon the filling mixture into each of the hollowed out bell peppers and transfer into slow cooker. Cook on "low" for 4 hours. Serve with optional toppings such as sour cream, freshly chopped cilantro, hot sauce, fresh lime wedges, etc.. Makes 4 servings.

Mock Kielbasa, Pineapple and Bean Medley

Ingredients:

1 yellow onion (rough chopped)

1 green bell pepper (seeded and rough chopped)

2 fresh garlic cloves (minced)

1 pound of vegetarian kielbasa (cut into sliced rounds)

3 cans (15 ounces each) pinto beans (rinsed and drained)

2 cups diced pineapple (if you don't have fresh pineapple, use one 20 ounce can - well drained)

1/2 cup of your favorite barbecue sauce

1/2 cup water

2 tablespoons prepared yellow mustard

2 tablespoons packed brown sugar

2 tablespoons red wine vinegar

pinch of ground black pepper

Combine all of the ingredients into your slow cooker. Stir very thoroughly to blend and cook on "low" for 6-7 hours. If mixture becomes too dry or thick, add in a little extra barbecue sauce or water to reach desired consistency. Taste and adjust seasonings as desired before serving as-is or over fresh steamed rice. Makes 6 servings.

Rice and Veggie Medley

Ingredients:

2-3 tablespoons olive oil

1 large yellow onion (diced)

2 large carrots (thinly sliced)

2 large celery stalks (diced)

5 fresh garlic cloves (minced)

4 cups vegetable broth

2 cups parboiled rice (dry measurement)

½ heaping cup finely chopped sun-dried tomatoes

½ teaspoon sea salt

½ teaspoon ground black pepper

½ teaspoon ground turmeric

1-1/2 cups peas (if using frozen, thaw first)

1 cup finely chopped red roasted peppers

½ cup finely chopped bell pepper (any variety; green, red, orange, yellow)

2 tablespoons fresh squeezed lemon juice

2 tablespoons freshly chopped parsley

Heat the olive oil in a skillet over medium heat. Once the oil is hot, add in the diced onion, carrots, celery and garlic and sauté while stirring continuously for 4-5 minutes. Add the sautéed vegetable medley into your slow cooker along with the vegetable broth, rice, chopped sun-dried tomatoes, sea salt, black pepper and turmeric. Stir to blend and cook on "low" for 4 hours or until all the rice is cooked and all of the liquid is absorbed.

Next, stir in the peas, chopped roasted peppers, chopped bell peppers and lemon juice and stir to blend. Increase heat setting to "high" and cook for a final 15 minutes. Serve the rice and veggie medley topped with the freshly chopped parsley. Makes 4-6 servings.

Marinara and Pesto Spinach Lasagna

Ingredients:

1 jar (24-26 ounces) of your favorite marinara sauce (I use one of the organic brands, Amy's, Newman's, Dave's)

3 fresh garlic cloves (minced)

2 teaspoons Italian seasoning blend

1 box of no-boil lasagna noodles

1 jar (usually 6-8 ounces) of basil or sundried tomato pesto sauce

1 container (15 ounce) ricotta cheese (I use Organic Valley)

1 large bunch of baby spinach

1 heaping cup of grated Parmesan cheese (fresh tastes best, but you can use the kind in a container as well)

16 ounces of shredded Mozzarella cheese

1/4 cup water

In a mixing bowl, whisk together the marinara sauce with the minced garlic and Italian seasoning blend. Evenly spoon 1/4 cup of the marinara sauce mixture into the bottom of your slow cooker. Add a layer of the no-boil lasagna noodles (you will have to break to pieces to fit) on top of the sauce, followed by a smear of ricotta cheese and pesto sauce. Add some of the baby spinach, followed by some of the Parmesan cheese and Mozzarella cheese.

Repeat the layering process until you run out of ingredients, while pressing down slightly with each layer. Once you've finished, slowly pour the 1/4 cup of water across the top and cover. Cook on "low" for 6-7 hours. You will know the lasagna is done when the top is golden brown and the cheese is bubbly, and the sides will pull away from the slow cooker. Uncover and let the lasagna rest for 10 minutes before serving. Makes 4-6 servings.

Tofu in Sweet and Spicy Peanut Sauce

Ingredients:

1 package of extra-firm tofu (pressed, drained and cubed)

1 tablespoon olive oil

1 tablespoon cornstarch (may also use all-purpose flour)

1/2 cup creamy style, natural peanut butter (no sugar added)

2 tablespoons Braggs liquid aminos (may also use Tamari or regular soy sauce)

2 tablespoons fresh squeezed lime juice

1 teaspoon fresh grated ginger root

3 fresh garlic cloves (minced)

1/4 teaspoon crushed red pepper flakes

1 large bunch of baby spinach (rough chopped)

*fresh steamed rice to serve on top of

Heat the olive oil in a skillet over medium heat. Once heated, whisk in the cornstarch (or flour) until well blended and then add in the cubed tofu. Saute while stirring frequently until tofu becomes lightly browned. Remove from heat.

Add the browned tofu along with all of the remaining ingredients EXCEPT the baby spinach into your slow cooker. Stir well to blend and cook on "low" for 4 hours. During the last 15 minutes of cooking time, stir in the baby spinach and recover. Once the spinach is fully wilted, serve as-is or over a bed of fresh steamed rice. Makes 4 servings if served over rice, or 2 servings if served as-is.

Fajitas Filling Mixture

Ingredients:

2 tablespoons olive oil

2 teaspoons ground cumin

2 teaspoons chili powder

1/2 teaspoon dried oregano

1/2 teaspoon garlic powder

4 large tomatoes (seeded and diced)

2 jalapeno peppers (seeded and cut into thin straw sticks)

2 large bell peppers (any variety - seeded and cut into thin straw sticks)

1 large yellow onion (cut into thin half rings)

* 1 can (15 ounce) black beans (warmed)

** 8 warmed flour toritillas

*** Suggested garnishes: fresh lime wedges; salsa or pico de gallo; sour cream (optional)

Whisk together the olive oil and spices in the bottom of your slow cooker. Add in all of the cut vegetables and toss until they are evenly coated and blended. Cook on "low" for 4-6 hours.

To assemble your fajitas, spread a dollop of the warmed black beans down the center of a warmed flour tortilla and top with some of the fajita filling. Serve with any, some or all of the suggested fajita garnishes. Makes enough filling to make 6-8 fajitas.

Burrito Filling Mixture

Ingredients:

2 cups vegetable broth

1 cup pearled barley (dry measurement)

1 can (15 ounce) black beans (rinsed and drained)

1 can (10 ounce) diced tomatoes with green chiles (with liquid)

1/3 cup diced onions

3/4 cup corn

1/4 cup diced black olives

3-4 fresh garlic cloves (minced)

1 tablespoon fresh squeezed lime juice

1-1/2 teaspoons chili powder

1 teaspoon ground cumin

1/2 teaspoon sea salt

1/4 teaspoon crushed red pepper flakes

1/4 cup fresh chopped cilantro

* 8 burrito size flour tortillas

* burrito toppings: shredded cheese; sour cream; pico de gallo; etc.

Combine all of the ingredients EXCEPT the chopped cilantro into your slow cooker. Stir well to blend and cook on "low" for 4-5 hours, until barley is tender and liquid is absorbed. Stir in the fresh chopped cilantro during the last 15 minutes of cooking time, and taste and adjust seasonings as desired.

Heat the flour tortillas in your oven, fill each with some of the burrito filling mixture and serve with your favorite burrito toppings. Makes 8 servings.

Taco Filling Mixture

Ingredients:

1 cup lentils (dry measurement)

1/2 cup quinoa (dry measurement)

4 cups vegetable broth

5 fresh garlic cloves (minced)

1 teaspoon chili powder

1 teaspoon ground cumin

1 teaspoon paprika

1/2 teaspoon dried oregano

1/2 teaspoon sea salt

1/4 teaspoon ground black pepper

* hard corn taco shells or soft flour tortillas

** your favorite taco toppings such as shredded cheese; salsa; diced onions; black olives; sour cream; fresh lime wedges

Rinse and thoroughly drain the dry lentils and quinoa.

Combine all of the ingredients in your slow cooker. Stir well to blend and cook on "low" for 8-10 hours. Taste and adjust seasonings as desired during the last 30 minutes of cooking time. Serve your taco filling in either hard corn shells or soft flour tortillas, along with all of your favorite taco toppings. Makes enough filling to make approximately 12 tacos.

Southwest Enchiladas

Ingredients:

1 can (15 ounce) black beans (rinsed and drained)

1 bunch of baby spinach (hand torn)

1 cup corn

1-2 fresh garlic cloves (minced)

1/2 teaspoon ground cumin

pinch of chili powder

pinch of sea salt

pinch of black pepper

8 ounces of shredded Cheddar, Colby or Mexican blended cheese (divided)

3-1/2 cups of your favorite salsa (divided)

8 corn tortillas (warmed in your oven to allow ease of rolling when prepping)

* toppings (optional): fresh lime wedges; diced green onions; sliced black olives; sour cream; shredded cabbage,

Using a fork, mash up the black beans in a mixing bowl. Once mashed, add in the hand torn baby spinach, corn, minced garlic, cumin, chili powder, sea salt, black pepper and HALF of the shredded Cheddar cheese. Stir well to evenly blend.

Evenly spoon the enchilada filling mixture onto the center of each of the 8 WARMED corn tortillas. (If you don't warm the tortillas, they will crack and split apart.) Spread HALF of the salsa into the bottom of your slow cooker. Carefully roll up each of the corn tortillas, and place seam-side down on top of the salsa layer in slow cooker. Arrange as tightly together as you can. Next, spoon the remaining salsa on top, followed by the remaining shredded Cheddar cheese. Cook on low for 3-4 hours. Serve with your favorite enchilada toppings and garnishes. Makes 4 servings of 2 enchiladas each.

Layered Italian Polenta and Bean Bake

Ingredients:

3 cans (15 ounces each) of either chickpeas or cannellini beans (rinsed and drained)

1 yellow onion (diced)

4-5 fresh garlic cloves (minced)

2 teaspoons Italian seasoning blend

1/4 cup basil pesto (divided)

1 tube (18 ounce) pre-cooked polenta (cut into 1-1/2 inch rounds)

2 cups of shredded Mozzarella or Italian cheese blend (divided)

1-1/2 to 2 cups diced tomatoes

2 cups hand torn baby spinach

arugula lettuce

In a mixing bowl, stir together the drained beans, diced onion, minced garlic, Italian seasoning blend and 2 Tablespoons of the pesto sauce until all ingredients are evenly combined.

Pour HALF of the bean mixture into the bottom of your slow cooker. Layer HALF of the sliced polenta rounds on top, followed by 1 cup of the shredded cheese. Top with all of the remaining bean mixture, followed by all of the remaining sliced polenta. Cook on "low" for 5-6 hours.

During the last 30 minutes of cooking time, top the cooked layers with the diced tomatoes, followed by the hand torn baby spinach and the remaining 1 cup of shredded cheese. Whisk together the remaining pesto with 1 tablespoon of water and drizzle on top. Let rest for 5-7 minutes before cutting and serving. Serve each serving on top of a pile of fresh arugula leaves. Makes 6-8 servings.

Asian Infused Tofu and Vegetables

Ingredients:

12-16 ounces of extra-firm tofu (pressed, excess water dried away, cubed)

1 tablespoon all-purpose flour

5 tablespoons olive oil (divided)

2 small yellow onions (diced)

5 fresh garlic cloves (minced)

2 teaspoons fresh grated ginger root

2 large carrots (cut into thin slices)

2-3 large celery stalks (diced)

2 cans (6 ounces each) sliced water chestnuts (drained)

1/2 teaspoon crushed red pepper flakes

2 tablespoons Braggs liquid aminos (may substitute with Tamari or regular soy sauce)

5-1/2 cups vegetable broth

8 ounces thinly sliced mushrooms (any variety, but I recommend shiitake or crimini for a more earthy flavor)

handful of snow peas (ends trimmed and rough chopped)

toasted sesame oil (to drizzle)

After prepping tofu (press, dry ultra-thoroughly and cubed), heat 2 tablespoons of the olive oil in a skillet over medium heat. Once the oil is heated, whisk in the flour until flour is fully dissolved into oil. Add in the cubed tofu and stir frequently while cooking until tofu becomes lightly browned, about 4-5 minutes. Remove from heat and set aside. Once cooled, transfer browned tofu into fridge. You will add it during the last hour of cooking.

Heat the remaining 3 tablespoon of olive oil in a skillet over medium heat. Add in the diced onion and saute until onion becomes translucent, about 4 minutes. Add in the minced garlic and ginger root and stir continuously until fragrant, about 30-60 seconds. Stir in the carrots, celery and water chestnuts, and continue cooking while stirring frequently for another 3-4 minutes.

Transfer the sauteed vegetable mixture into your slow cooker, and all in all of the remaining ingredients EXCEPT the browned tofu (keep in fridge until ready to add), mushrooms, snow peas and sesame oil. Stir well to blend and cook on "low" 6-8 hours. Add in the browned tofu, sliced mushrooms and snow peas during the last 1 hour of cooking time. When ready to serve, ladle into individual serving bowls as-is or over a bed of fresh steamed rice and drizzle each serving with a small amount of the roasted sesame oil. Makes 8 servings.

Creole Jambalaya

Ingredients:

2 tablespoons olive oil

1 yellow onion (diced)

4-5 fresh garlic cloves (minced)

1 green bell pepper (seeded and diced)

3 large celery stalks (diced)

1-1/2 cups vegetable broth

1 tablespoon miso paste

8 ounces of vegan sausage (rough chopped into bite size pieces)

8 ounces seitan (rough chopped into bite size pieces)

2 cups diced tomatoes

1/2 tablespoon Creole spice blend (more or less, to taste)

1 teaspoon dried thyme

1 teaspoon dried oregano

* fresh steamed rice to serve Jambalaya on

** fresh chopped parsley

*** hot sauce and/or crushed red pepper flakes, for added heat (optional)

Heat the olive oil in a skillet over medium heat. Add in the onions and saute until onions become translucent, about 4 minutes. Add in the minced garlic and stir continuously until fragrant, about 30-60 seconds. Add in the diced bell pepper and celery and cook while stirring continuously for an additional 2-3 minutes.

Transfer the sauteed vegetable mixture into your slow cooker along with all of the remaining ingredients. Stir well to blend and cook on "low" for 4-6 hours. Taste and adjust seasonings as desired, and if you desire more "heat" to your jambalaya then you can add in some hot sauce or crushed red pepper flakes at this time. When ready, serve in a bowl over a scoop of fresh steamed rice and sprinkle with some fresh chopped parsley. Makes 4 servings.

German Style Mock Sausage, Sauerkraut and Potatoes

Ingredients:

1 pound vegan kielbasa (sliced)

4 large golden russet potatoes (peeled and cut into large cubes)

4 cups of sauerkraut (with liquid)

1 teaspoon caraway seeds

1 teaspoon ground black pepper

1/2 teaspoon sea salt

* fresh chopped parsley for garnish

Crush the caraway seeds with a rolling pin or spice grinder to release the aromatic essential oils. Combine all of the ingredients in your slow cooker. Stir well to blend and cook on "low" for 5-7 hours. * If using homemade sauerkraut, add in 3/4 cup of water.

Serve with a sprinkling of fresh chopped parsley. Makes 6 servings.

Lentil Barbeque

Ingredients:

2-3 tablespoons olive oil

1 large yellow onion (diced)

1-2 fresh garlic cloves (minced)

1 large bell pepper, any variety (seeded and diced)

2-3 teaspoons chili powder

1-1/2 cups lentils (dry measurement - soak for 30 minutes, rinse and drain before using)

1-1/2 cups diced tomatoes

3-1/2 cups vegetable broth

2 tablespoons Braggs liquid aminos (may also use Tamari or regular soy sauce)

2 tablespoons brown sugar

drizzle of apple cider vinegar or balsamic vinegar

1 tablespoon yellow mustard

1 teaspoon sea salt

1/2 teaspoon ground black pepper

* Optional barbeque sandwich toppings/sides: shredded slaw; sliced pickles; sliced tomatoes; sliced onions, etc.

Heat the olive oil in a skillet over medium heat. Add in the diced onion and saute until onion becomes translucent, about 4 minutes. Add in the minced garlic and stir continuously until fragrant, about 30-60 seconds. Add in the diced bell peppers and chili powder and stir continuously while cooking for an additional 1-2 minutes.

Transfer the sauteed vegetable mixture into your slow cooker along with all of the remaining ingredients. Stir well to blend. Cook on "low" for 8-10 hours. Stir well before serving and adjust any seasonings as desired. Serve on your favorite healthy bun for a delicious barbeque sandwich, along with your favorite barbeque sandwich toppings and sides. Makes 4-6 servings.

Lentil and Vegetable Stroganoff

Ingredients:

4 tablespoons olive oil

2 yellow onions (diced)

6 large carrots (thinly sliced)

6 large celery stalks (diced)

4-5 fresh garlic cloves (minced)

1 tablespoon tomato paste

1/4 cup balsamic vinegar

1 tablespoon brown mustard

1 large (or 2 medium) golden russet potato (peeled and thinly sliced)

2 cups lentils (dry measurement - rinsed and drained well before using)

4 cups (32 ounces) vegetable broth (may also use a vegetarian mock beef broth)

1-1/2 teaspoons sea salt

1 teaspoon ground black pepper

1 pound bunch of fresh spinach (stems removed and rough chopped)

* fresh chopped parsley for garnish

Heat the olive oil in a skillet over medium heat. Add in the diced onions, carrots and celery and saute while stirring frequently for 5 minutes. Add in the minced garlic, tomato paste, balsamic vinegar and brown mustard and cook for an additional 2 minutes while stirring continuously.

Transfer the sauteed vegetable mixture into your slow cooker along with all of the remaining ingredients EXCEPT the spinach. Stir well to blend and cook on "low" for 8-10 hours. Stir in the chopped spinach during the last 30 minutes of cooking time. Taste and adjust seasonings as desired and serve with a sprinkle of fresh chopped parsley. Makes 6 servings.

Zesty Barbeque Tofu

Ingredients:

2 packages (13 ounces each) extra-firm tofu (pressed, excess water patted dry and cubed)

1-1/2 cups vegan ketchup

4 tablespoons brown sugar

2 tablespoons Braggs liquid aminos (may also use Tamari or regular soy sauce)

1 tablespoon apple cider vinegar

1 tablespoon crushed red pepper flakes (more or less, to heat preference)

1 teaspoon garlic powder

pinch of ground black pepper

* 4-6 warm steamed or grilled buns to serve barbeque on

In a large mixing bowl, stir together all of the ingredients EXCEPT the cubed tofu until well combined. Add in the cubed tofu and gently toss until evenly coated. Transfer mixture into your slow cooker and cook on "low" for 4-6 hours. Serve on warm steamed or grilled buns along with your favorite barbeque side dish. Makes 4-6 servings.

Creamy Artichoke Linguine

Ingredients:

4-1/2 cups diced tomatoes

2 jars (14 ounces each) artichoke hearts (drained and chopped)

6 fresh garlic cloves (minced)

1 cup vegetable broth

1 tablespoon Italian seasoning blend

1 teaspoon sea salt

1 teaspoon ground black pepper

1/2 cup heavy whipping cream

* 1 pound box (16 ounces) of cooked linguine noodles to serve creamy artichoke sauce over

* fresh chopped parsley for garnish

Lightly oil the bottom and sides of your slow cooker with olive oil. Combine all of the ingredients into your slow cooker EXCEPT the heavy whipping cream and linguine noodles. Stir well to blend and cook on "low" for 6-7 hours. Stir in the heavy whipping cream during the last 30 minutes of cooking time. You also want to cook your linguine during the final 30 minutes of cooking time. Taste and adjust seasonings as desired and serve creamy artichoke sauce over fresh cooked linguine noodles sprinkled with some fresh chopped parsley. Makes 6 servings.

Sweet and Tangy Mock Barbecue Beef

Ingredients:

4 bags (12 ounces each) veggie crumbles (I use MorningStar or LightLife Smart Ground)

1 large yellow onion (diced)

1 large green bell pepper (seeded and diced)

1-1/2 cups of your favorite barbecue sauce

1/2 cup vegetable broth

1/2 cup apricot preserves

1 heaping tablespoon brown mustard

1 tablespoon packed brown sugar

* your favorite buns to serve the mock barbecue beef on

Combine all of the ingredients into your slow cooker. Stir very thoroughly to blend, and cook on "low" for 6 hours. If barbecue mixture becomes too thick, you can add in a little extra barbecue sauce, apricot preserves, or vegetable broth to reach desired consistency. Give the mixture a good stir a few times during cooking time. Serve the barbecue on buns along with your favorite barbecue sides. Makes 8-10 servings.

Veggie Spaghetti Sauce

Ingredients:

4 tablespoons olive oil

1-1/2 large yellow onions (diced)

5 fresh garlic cloves

7 cups diced tomatoes

2 cups tomato sauce

3 large bell peppers (any variety, seeded and diced)

3 zucchini (peeled and diced)

3 cups diced mushrooms (any variety)

2 tablespoons Italian seasoning blend

2 teaspoons sea salt

2 teaspoon ground black pepper

2 large bay leaves

* 2 pounds of fresh cooked pasta to serve veggie spaghetti sauce over (or to toss with)

Heat the olive oil in a skillet over medium heat. Add in the diced onions and saute until onions become translucent, about 4 minutes. Add in the minced garlic and stir continuously until fragrant, about 30-60 seconds. Transfer the sauteed onion-garlic mixture into your slow cooker along with all of the remaining ingredients. Stir well to blend and cook on "low" for 6-8 hours. Remove bay leaves and taste and adjust seasonings as desired. Serve over fresh cooked pasta of your choice. Makes 10-12 servings.

German Style Sausage and Sauerkraut

Ingredients:

1 package (14 ounce) of vegan kielbasa (I use Tofurky brand)

2 large green variety apples (cored and cut into thin wedge slices)

1 large yellow onion (cut into thin half ring slices)

1 small jar of sauerkraut (I use about half of a 32 ounce jar of Eden organic sauerkraut)

2 tablespoons caraway seeds

1 tablespoon raw sugar

sea salt and black pepper (to taste)

You can either keep the vegan kielbasa as whole sausages, or cut them into 1/2 inch thick round slices.

Combine all of the ingredients into your slow cooker. Stir well to blend and cook on "low" for 6-7 hours. Makes 4 servings.

Mock Chickn' and Dumplings

Ingredients:

1 large yellow onion (diced)

2 fresh garlic cloves (minced)

2 large carrots (sliced)

2 large celery stalks (diced)

1/2 cup diced green bell pepper

1-1/2 pounds of vegetarian chicken strips (rough chopped - I use 3 bags of LightLife brand)

3 cups vegetable broth

1-2 teaspoons of Table seasoning blend

1/2 teaspoon sea salt

1/2 teaspoon ground black pepper

2 cups vegan biscuit mix

2/3 cups plain milk (regular or non-dairy)

Combine all of the ingredients in your slow cooker EXCEPT the biscuit mix and milk. Stir well to blend and cook on "low" for 6-8 hours. Whisk together the biscuit mix and milk in a mixing bowl to form a batter. During the last 1 hour of cooking time, increase your slow cooker temperature to "high" and drop the batter by spoonfuls into your slow cooker WITHOUT stirring to make your dumplings. Taste and adjust seasonings as desired before serving with a sprinkle of fresh chopped parsley. Makes 4 servings.

Seitan Italian "Beef" Sandwiches

Ingredients:

1-1/2 pounds seitan (very thinly sliced)

3 cups vegetable broth

2 large green bell peppers (seeded and cut into thin julienne strips)

4 fresh garlic cloves (minced)

3 tablespoons Italian giardiniera peppers (plus more for serving, as desired)

2 teaspoons fennel seed

2 teaspoons dried oregano

1 teaspoon sea salt

1/2 teaspoon ground black pepper

* 6 Italian or French rolls to serve on

Combine all of the ingredients in your slow cooker. Stir well to blend and cook on "low" for 6-7 hours, stirring every few hours if possible. Serve of toasted or steamed Italian or French bread rolls. Sandwich tastes even better with a couple spoonfuls of au jus poured over it. Makes 6 servings.

Mock Italian Sausage and Feta Cheese Stuffed Peppers

Ingredients:

4 green or red bell peppers

1/2 cup couscous (dry measurement)

3/4 cup water

4 ounces of vegetarian Italian sausage (diced - I use Field Roast Italian seasoned)

1/2 cup finely crumbled herbed Feta cheese (divided)

2 tablespoons finely diced onions

1/4 teaspoon sea salt

1/4 teaspoon ground black pepper

2 tablespoons fresh chopped basil

Prep the bell peppers by slicing off their tops and carefully spooning out their seeds and innards and then set aside.

Bring the 3/4 cup water to a boil in a saucepan over medium heat. Stir in the couscous, remove from heat, cover pan and let the couscous stand for 5-7 minutes to absorb the water. Once water has been absorbed, fluff the couscous with a fork.

In a mixing bowl, combine the couscous, diced vegetarian sausage, the crumbled Feta cheese (RESERVING 2 tablespoons of the Feta cheese), diced onions, sea salt and black pepper, and toss to evenly combine all ingredients. Evenly stuff the filling mixture into the 4 prepped bell peppers and arrange into the bottom of your slow cooker. Cook on "low" for 4-6 hours, until peppers are nice and tender. Serve each one with a sprinkle of the reserved 2 tablespoons of crumbled Feta cheese and the fresh chopped basil. Makes 4 servings.

Sweet and Sour Chick'n

Ingredients:

1/3 cup raw sugar

1/3 cup ketchup

1/4 cup orange juice

3 tablespoons cornstarch

2 tablespoons apple cider vinegar

2 tablespoons Braggs liquid aminos (may also use Tamari or regular soy sauce)

1 tablespoon fresh grated ginger root

1 yellow onion (rough chopped)

1 large green bell pepper (seeded and rough chopped)

1 large red bell pepper (seeded and rough chopped)

1-1/2 cups diced pineapple (if not using fresh, use 2 - 8 ounce cans, well drained)

1 pound of vegetarian chick'n meat (chopped - I use LightLife Smart Strips)

* about 3 cups of fresh steamed rice to serve over

In a mixing bowl, whisk together the raw sugar, ketchup, orange juice, cornstarch, vinegar, liquid aminos and grated ginger until well combined. Transfer the sauce mixture into your slow cooker along with all of the remaining ingredients. Stir to blend and cook on "low" for 6 hours. If mixture becomes too thick, stir in a little extra orange juice. Serve over fresh steamed rice. Makes 4-6 servings.

Slow Cooker Cooking Tips

1. Like all kitchen appliances and gadgets, each is unique. Therefore, get to know your slow cooker, and whether it tends to run on the hot side or the cool side. For whatever reason, brand new slow cookers tend to cook on the slightly hotter side, which means that recipe cooking times are generally reduced. This is more typically with smaller sized slow cookers vs. their larger counterparts.

2. Just like cooking on a stovetop, the called for liquid content (water, vegetable broth, tomato sauce, etc.) may need to be adjusted to adjust for too thick soups, stews, chilis, etc.

3. Most of the recipes in this slow cooker cookbook are for 4-8 servings. If you are just cooking for yourself or you and one other, generally you can cut a recipe in half, which will also typically reduce cooking time, with the exception of the desserts.

4. Many of the recipes call for vegetable broth. You can always use plain filtered water in place of the vegetable broth BUT this will greatly alter the taste profile of the dish, since the vegetable broth is loaded with natural veggie flavors. If you do decide to swap out water in place of vegetable broth in a recipe, I highly recommend increasing the amount of spices and seasonings to prevent your dish from turning out too bland.

5. Many of the recipes call for a quick sauté of onions, or onions and garlic, or onions-garlic-chopped veggies prior to combining all of the ingredients into your slow cooker. You can always skip this step, but this will definitely alter the final flavor outcome of your dish, just like substituting

water in place of vegetable broth. Doing a quick sauté before combining all of your ingredients takes less than 5 minutes, and the results are very well worth it.

6. The recipes in this cookbook call for a mix of dry beans and pre-cooked canned beans. If you tend to cook all of your own beans, for any recipe calling for a single 15 ounce can of beans, you would replace that with 1-1/2 cups of cooked beans.

7. Another highly recommended touch to many of the recipes, is the final addition of fresh chopped herbs. Fresh chopped parsley, cilantro and dill are cheap to grow or buy and the freshness of the herbs really make your just prepared slow cooker recipe pop with flavor.

8. When using canned beans, I do recommend using organic as much as you possibly can.

9. If you have a slow cooker with a removable insert, as most do, another tip is to fully prep and assemble your ingredients into your slow cooker insert the night before and store it in the fridge. Take the insert out to rest at room temperature for 30 minutes (or until the insert has come to room temperature), and then plug it in and set it to the called for heat and cooking time. This is great for busy mornings.

10. Do not to lift the lid during cooking time unless a recipe specifically calls for stirring. Heat quickly escapes and reduces the slow cooker temperature every time you take a peek unnecessarily. If a recipe does call for a stir during cooking time, do it quickly without fully opening the lid.

11. The majority of the recipes in this slow cooker cookbook call for cooking on "low" heat. Here is a general guideline to use if you wish to speed up the cooking time. "Low" for 4-6 hours = "High" for 1-1/2 to 2 hours. "Low" for 6-10 hours = "High" for 3-4 hours. And, most importantly, "warm" is not a cooking temperature.

12. High altitudes (generally over 5000 feet), calls for longer cooking time. Plan on adding 20-30 minutes to every hour in a called for recipe if you live at a high altitude, and this primarily is the case when a base ingredient in a slow cooker recipe is beans.

13. You can thicken a recipe and concentrate its flavors by removing the lid and increasing the heat to "high" during the last 30 minutes of cooking time. This is great for soups, stews, chilis and some miscellaneous main meal recipes, but I don't recommend it for desserts, most appetizers and breakfast recipes.

14. Never fill your slow cooker more than ¾ of the way full. Your ingredients won't cook evenly, and the end result will typically be poor. Again, mind your serving size, listed recipe ingredient size and slow cooker size, and adjust accordingly for optimal results.

15. When a recipe has come to the end of the cooking time and you're not quite ready to serve it, switch the heat setting to "low". This is also recommended when cooking appetizers in a slow cooker. Most appetizers are served warm, yet you don't want the recipe to continue cooking, therefore, if you are planning on serving the appetizer straight from the slow cooker, immediately lower the heat setting to "warm" right before serving.

Available Books by Author:

Easy Vegetarian Cooking: 100 – 5 Ingredients or Less, Easy & Delicious Vegetarian Recipes

Natural Foods: 100-5- Ingredients or Less, Raw Food Recipes for Every Meal Occasion

Easy Vegetarian Cooking: 75 Delicious Vegetarian Casserole Recipes

Easy Vegetarian Cooking: 75 Delicious Vegetarian Soup and Stew Recipes

The Veggie Goddess Vegetarian Cookbook Collection: Volumes 1-4

Easy Vegan Cooking: 100 Easy and Delicious Vegan Recipes

Vegan Cooking: 50 Delectable Vegan Dessert Recipes

Holiday Vegan Recipes: Holiday Menu Planning for Halloween through New Years

The Veggie Goddess Vegan Cookbook Collection: Volumes 1-3

Natural Cures: 200 All Natural Fruit & Veggie Remedies for Weight Loss, Health and Beauty

Healthy Living: How to Purify Your Body in a Polluted World

Gluten Free Bread: 100 Wheat-Free Bread and Baked Goods Recipes

100 – 5 Ingredients or Less Quick and Easy Vegetarian Recipes (Volume 2)

Slow Cooker Recipes: 200 Healthy Vegetarian Slow Cooker Recipes

About The Author

Gina 'The Veggie Goddess' Matthews, resides in sunny Phoenix, Arizona, and has been a lover of animals, nature, gardening, natural living and, of course, vegetarian and vegan cuisine since childhood. 'The Veggie Goddess' strongly encourages home gardening, supporting your local farmers and organic food co-ops, preserving the well-being of Mother Earth, and supporting and protecting animal rights.

http://www.theveggiegoddess.com

http://www.facebook.com/theveggiegoddess

http://www.pinterest.com/veggiegoddess

Printed in Great Britain
by Amazon